Text by Michael Head
Colour Artwork by Chris Warner

Revised New Edition
First Published 1977.

ISBN 0 85524 011 3

Distributed in the U.S.A. by
Squadron/Signal Publications Inc.,
3461 East Ten Mile Road,
Warren, Michigan 48091.

Printed in Great Britain by
Staples Printers Ltd.,
Trafalgar Road, Kettering,
Northamptonshire,
for the publishers, Almark Publishing Co. Ltd.
49 Malden Way, New Malden,
Surrey KT3 6EA, England.

INTRODUCTION

This publication presents in one volume a comprehensive account of the French Artillery forces of the First Empire period. It illustrates and describes the guns and auxiliary transport equipment as well as the artillery arms and their uniforms of the campaigns which culminated in the Battle of Waterloo, 1815. French uniforms and dress regulations of the Napoleonic era were immensely complex, in the artillery no less than in the other arms. The book covers the years 1804-1815 and all changes in uniform detail are recorded. Where possible, descriptions of uniform in the text are keyed to the appropriate colour illustration or drawing. Thus it is possible to find the drawing quickly from the plate and reference letter. all the drawings of guns and transport vehicles are reproduced to 1:30 scale, specially for the modeller working with the standard 54-55mm size minature soldier figures.

Sincere thanks are due to Lynn Sangster of Historex Agents for his continued encouragement and assistance with the researches for this book. Thanks are also due to Frank Hinchliffe of Hinchliffe Models for the information on the unusual ambulances shown in the book.

Lastly the author must thank his wife whose help in typing the draft manuscript was invaluable.

PART 1:   Artillery Equipment, 1804-1815

French guns were designed on the Gribeauval system developed in 1776. The drawbacks to this system were that the carriages were heavy and the gunners all marched on foot (instead of riding on the limber and gun as in the British system) and also that some guns had to be moved from the rear trunnion travelling position to the front trunnion for firing.

The cannon were named from the weight of their projectiles, so we have pieces of 12, 8 and 4, indicating weights in pounds (lbs) respectively. There were also 8 and 6 inch bore howitzers. Bronze cannon were mounted on two wheeled wooden carriages. The heavier 12 and 8 pdrs had two positions for the trunnions, the front for firing and the rear when travelling to help balance the weight of the gun. The limbers were also two wheeled with a pintle spike fitting into a metal hole on the trail transom of the carriage.

Cannon fired solid balls, or cannister containing lead bullets. Effective ranges were approximately 800-900 metres for a 12 pdr, 800 metres for an 8 pdr and 700 metres for a 4 pdr. When using cannister the ranges were 600, 550 and 400 metres.

Howitzers fired a round shell filled with gun powder and with a fuse to explode between 1,200 and 700 metres. When the shells exploded the effective radius was around 20 metres. The balls were about 2mm smaller than the bore of the gun. The ball was secured by two tin straps crossing each other to a wooden sabot or shoe which was scooped out to allow about a quarter of the ball to fit. A serge bag was then filled with powder and the neck fastened to the wooden shoe tying into a groove. The cannister was a tin cylinder filled with lead balls which was attached to a wooden shoe.

Provision was made for about 300 to 350 charges per gun and these were carried in the trail chests, caissons and park wagons. The 4 pdrs usually had two caissons, 8 pdrs three, and 12 pdrs and howitzers, five. Caissons also carried matches and gun powder. As well as gun ammunition, infantry cartridges were carried, and the park and divisional wagons carried pickaxes, wheels and artificers' tools, etc. There was also pontoon and mobile forge equipment.

On the march, horse artillery men followed their piece riding in two files. The foot artillery crew however marched on either side of their gun. The guns would be at the head of a company column, followed by the caissons, park wagons were usually to be found in the rear of the column.

When marching with the army the foot artillery would maintain the pace of the column. This varied depending on the terrain and the urgency of the movement. The average was 2½ miles an hour and at the most four miles an hour. Horse artillery operating alone or in conjunction with cavalry could be expected to increase these figures by 20 to 30 per cent. A single gun could be unlimbered and ready to fire in less than a minute given favourable conditions. It took from one to three minutes to limber up and move from a firing position.

The number of men to serve a cannon varied but the following gives a basic example. With a 4 pdr weapon, 8 men formed the gun team of whom 5 were specialists. The remainder were used to haul the gun into position, etc, and bring up ammunition. With an 8 pdr or 6 inch howitzer 13 men formed the team with 8 specialists. The 12 pdr needed 15 men, of whom 8 were specialists.

Firing procedure

The firing procedure was as follows: The vent hole in the breech was blocked and the gun was sighted, using the screw to raise or lower the muzzle. The barrel was then swabbed out with water and a sponge to clear burnt powder from the previous discharge. the cartridge (ball or cannister, shoe and powder bag) was then rammed down on top of a packing wad which utilized material immediately to hand, usually grass or hay. The vent hole was then unstopped and cleaned with a priming wire. This had a pointed iron tip which pierced the powder bag. A primer was then inserted through the vent hole and consisted of a reed containing inflammable impregnated cotton and which carried the flame to the powder. Either a portefire which burned for about 10 minutes or a linstock, which was a long pole with the match wound around the top and clamped, was then applied to the primer and the gun discharged.

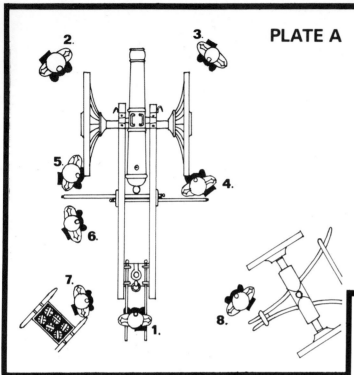

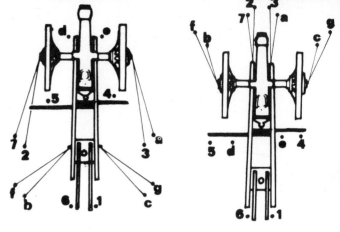

Diagram showing positions and functions of gun crew and helpers; the numbers are keyed to the descriptions in text.

In action, the ammunition chest would be placed at the rear and to one side of the trail and a caisson would be positioned about 30 metres to the rear of the gun. The horses and limber would also move back about 30 metres. In the case of horse artillery, the train drivers usually remained mounted and held the reins of the gun crew's horses. Between each gun a space of approximately 20 metres was allowed.

Gun crew duties

Plate A above shows the positions of a gun team with their infantry helpers in firing position, pulling the gun forwards and backwards. The following descriptions of their duties are keyed by the numbers to the drawing:

1. Gunner 1st Class or Corporal

In action. He gives the command 'Load' (*Chargez*), aims the gun with the help of the levers thrust through the rings on the transom, he then moves to the right, or left, to observe the effect of the shot. When moving the gun forward he held the right hand lever in two hands, when moving back it was held with one hand.

2. Gunner 1st Class. Porte Ecouvillon.

He held the *ecouvillon* (sponge on a rod) which was used to clean the gun of burnt powder after firing. When the cartridge was placed in the muzzle he rammed it home with the other end of the *ecouvillon*. He then stood on the left of the gun. Moving forward he pulled a strap attached to the hook on the left hand side of the carriage and when retreating the gun, the strap was attached to the hook on the axle end.

3. Gunner 1st class Chargeur.

On the command 'Chargez' he assists 2 to sponge out the barrel then receives the cartridge from 7, places it in the muzzle and stands off to the right. When moving the piece forwards or backwards he had the same role as 2, but on the right hand side.

4. Gunner.

This man was in charge of the matches and carried a match (porte fire) or a linstock (a pole with a match wound around the top and clamped into position) in his right hand.

In action he has the bucket of water nearby and actually fires the gun. Moving the gun to the front or rear he pushes on a lever inserted through the 'U' brackets above the trail.

5. Gunner.

This man carried a pouch of primer tubes on a waistbelt and a pointed 'pin' in his right hand. Moving to the front or back he fulfilled the same function as 4 but on the left hand side. In action it was he who pierced the cartridge bag by pushing the pin down the vent hole and placed a primer tube (see plate P) into the vent. He then gave the order to fire.

6. Gunner 1st Class

When moving forward or backward he did the same as 1 but on the left side. On the command 'Chargez' he stopped up the vent hole with the thumb of his left hand, (usually covered by a leather finger stall) to prevent the ignition of un-burnt powder, when the sponge and charge were rammed home, by the rush of air through the vent. At the same time with his right hand, he operated the elevating screw.

7. Gunner Pourvoyeur.

He stood to the rear of the trail and carried the cartridge to 3. When moving the piece he did the same as 2.

8.

This man stood by the limber and should the need arise, he replaced or helped any of the other gunners.

a, b, c, d, e, f, g

These were infantrymen detailed to help with the movement of the gun. In action they helped supply the ammunition from the caissons and could if need be take the place of the gunners. In action these infantrymen fell in in two rows of four well clear of the trail at rear and facing its axis.

Battery composition

The size of the artillery contingent within a specific command, ie division, corps etc, is impossible to define. They were allocated when and where necessary. At regimental level there existed at various times small numbers of 4 or 6 pdr guns, usually captured from the enemy and manned by infantrymen.

The composition of batteries varied but in general was as follows: Horse companies usually consisted of six guns composed of two 6 inch howitzers (with long barrels) and six 12 pdrs, or two 6 inch howitzers (short barrels) and six 8 pdrs. The latter predominated. In the Guard Artillery the Young Guard companies usually consisted of a battery of eight 4 pdrs.

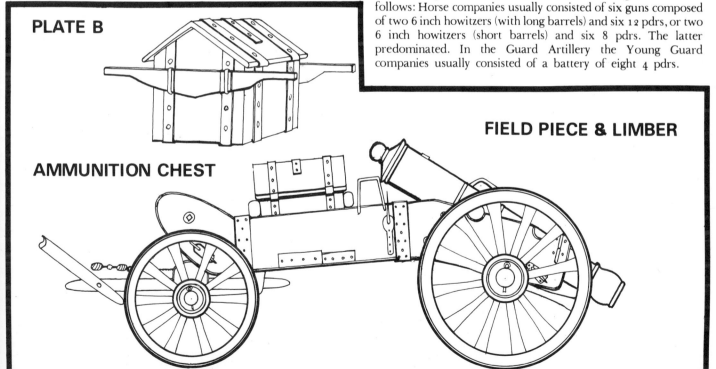

PLATE B

AMMUNITION CHEST

FIELD PIECE & LIMBER

Gribeauval system guns

The drawings show (see plate C/1 & D) the inherent simplicity of the Gribeauval system whereby guns of different calibres were carried on standard types of carriage. The gun carriages had trails composed of two straight frames almost parallel to each other, but narrowing slightly to the rear.

An ammunition chest was carried, supported by its handles, between the trail frames when the gun was limbered up. When in action the chest was either placed near the gun or rested on the 'A' frame of the limber.

Howitzers (6 and 8 inch) had a slightly different carriage with only one trunnion rest, but otherwise the carriage was very similar to that of the 8 and 12 pdr cannons.

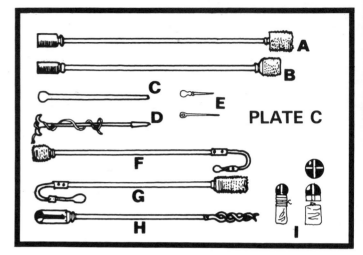

PLATE C

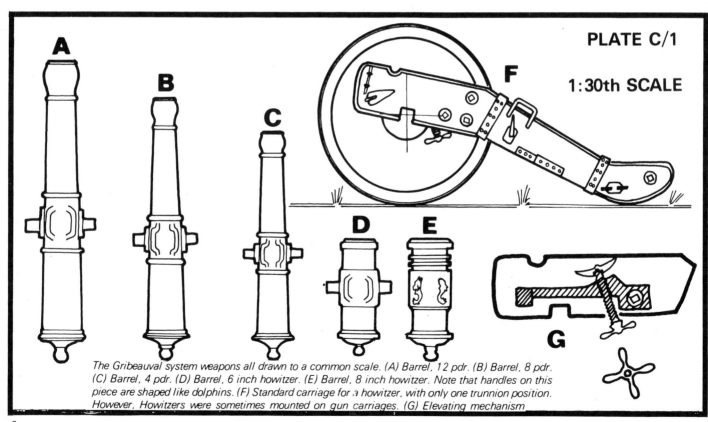

PLATE C/1

1:30th SCALE

The Gribeauval system weapons all drawn to a common scale. (A) Barrel, 12 pdr. (B) Barrel, 8 pdr. (C) Barrel, 4 pdr. (D) Barrel, 6 inch howitzer. (E) Barrel, 8 inch howitzer. Note that handles on this piece are shaped like dolphins. (F) Standard carriage for a howitzer, with only one trunnion position. However, Howitzers were sometimes mounted on gun carriages. (G) Elevating mechanism

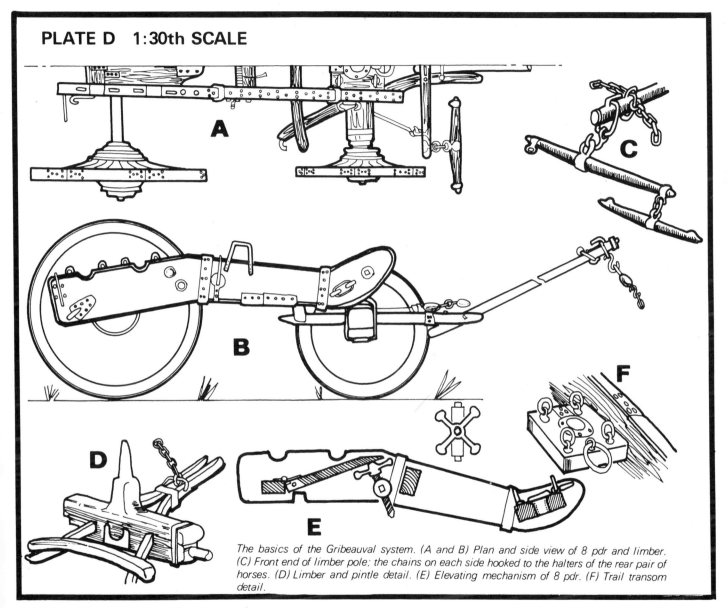

PLATE D   1:30th SCALE

The basics of the Gribeauval system. (A and B) Plan and side view of 8 pdr and limber. (C) Front end of limber pole; the chains on each side hooked to the halters of the rear pair of horses. (D) Limber and pintle detail. (E) Elevating mechanism of 8 pdr. (F) Trail transom detail.

TOP LEFT

(A) Rammer and sponge for 12 pdr gun. (B) Rammer and sponge for 8 pdr gun. (C and D) Linstocks. (E) Primer ́pins ́. (F) Crooked handle sponge and rammer, Horse Artillery. (G) Crooked handle sponge and rammer, 4 pdr gun. (H) Worm and ladle, Light Troop. (I) Cartridges for 8 inch and 6 inch howitzers.

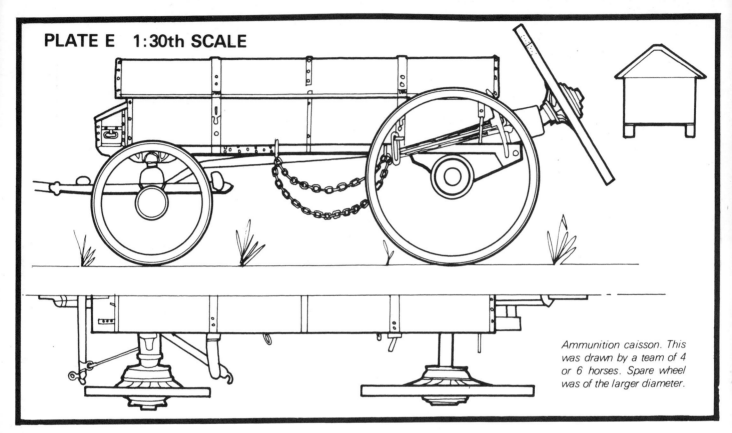

PLATE E   1:30th SCALE

Ammunition caisson. This was drawn by a team of 4 or 6 horses. Spare wheel was of the larger diameter.

AMMUNITION CAISSON

PLATE F

Colour of guns and limbers

The guns and limbers were painted an olive green colour with the metal strappings and fixtures painted black. The actual shade of olive green is difficult to define precisely but appears to have been mainly brown with a greenish cast from the evidence of surviving paint chippings. Records exist which give the information that the colour of the guns was obtained by using a mixture of yellow ochre and black in the ratio of approximately 80:1.

Train wagons

Supporting the gun batteries were many forms of wagons and ambulances, and the main types are illustrated on the following pages.

Ammunition caisson

This was a long narrow-bodied wagon with the sloping top hinged to open, and the interior divided into compartments for ammunition. The front wheel unit of the caisson was identical with the limber of the guns, and four or six horses were used to pull it. A spare wheel, usually the larger variety, was carried at the rear and shovels and a pick fastened on the side. A detachable tool box was carried at the front. Colour was olive green with black iron work.

With the Army of the Rhine, the ammunition caisson appeared in a new guise in the service of the medical corps. Pulled by four horses, the caisson had a wooden seat at the front and the 'lid' was padded and covered by black leather. A foot board was

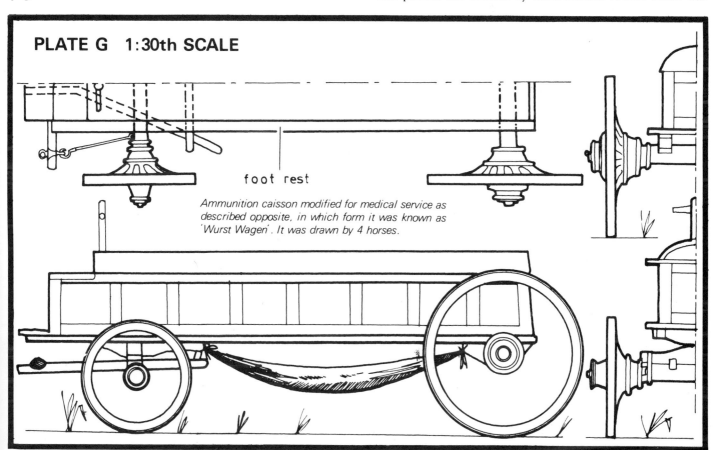

PLATE G   1:30th SCALE

foot rest

Ammunition caisson modified for medical service as described opposite, in which form it was known as 'Wurst Wagen'. It was drawn by 4 horses.

added on each side and a wooden cross rose from the front of the lid. A canvas hammock was slung underneath to carry loose articles. Surgeons and medical orderlies sat astride the top, as on a horse, and held on to the forward man's waist. The foremost man held on to the cross.

This modified type of caisson provided rapid transport for the surgeons as well as carrying medical surgical supplies. Documentation mentions a cover to protect the riders from rain or sun but no evidence remains of the form that it took. Known as the *Wurst Wagen* by the artillery men of Austria and Bavaria (ie, 'Sausage cart') by reason of its long, narrow shape, it came to be

known universally as such. The *Wurst Wagen* disappeared from service around 1810. It had been evolved by Percy who with Larrey designed most of the medical transport in service with the French Army.

Light ambulance

It was in 1797 that Larrey formed the *Legion Volante* with the Army of Italy, this consisted of three divisions, each of 12 light wagons and four heavy wagons. Of the 12 light wagons, eight

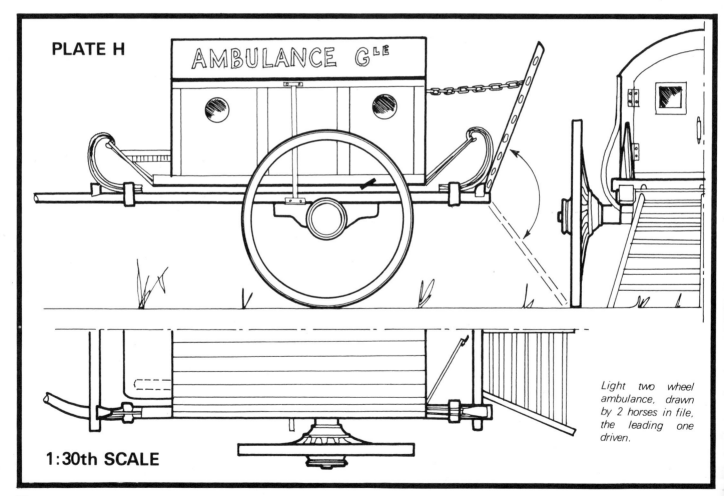

PLATE H

AMBULANCE G^{LE}

1:30th SCALE

Light two wheel ambulance, drawn by 2 horses in file, the leading one driven.

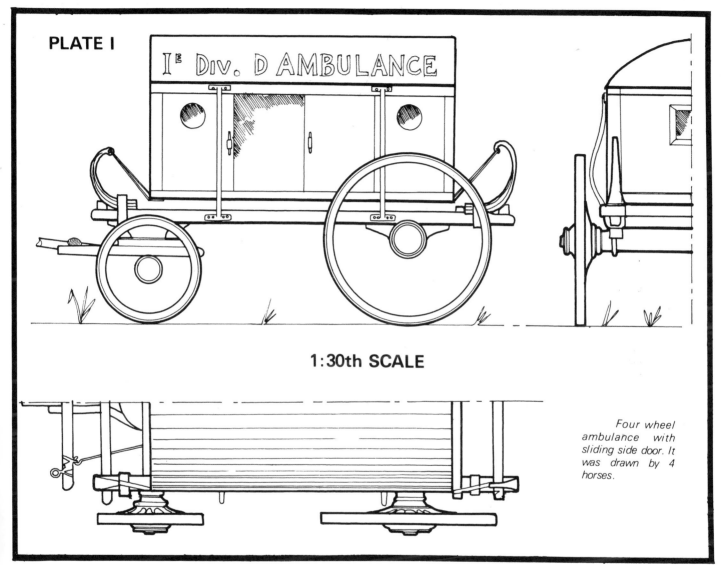

PLATE I

I DIV. D AMBULANCE

1:30th SCALE

Four wheel ambulance with sliding side door. It was drawn by 4 horses.

were two wheeled and four were four wheeled. The first was driven by two horses, the foremost one being ridden by a driver of the *Train d'Equipage* and could carry two wounded men. The floor was padded and two stretchers rested on a frame. Around the inside, pockets were provided for bandages, etc. The second type was useful when the terrain was more difficult and was drawn by four horses. Four wounded could be carried and the

ambulance was unusual in that sliding doors were provided on the left side. The front wheel unit appears to be a variation on the standard limber. Both these Larrey ambulances were well sprung, as can be seen from the plans, following the practice in use at that time for private carriages. Page 12 shows a delightful ambulance of the Imperial Guard with its leather canopy and side lamps.

PLATE J

1:30th SCALE

AMBULANCE GARDE IMPERIALE

Special ambulance of the Imperial Guard, a non-standard type.

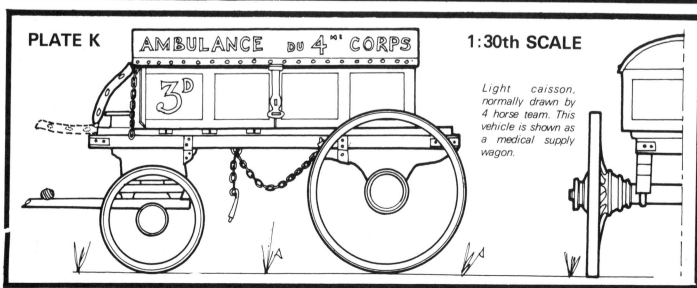

PLATE K

1:30th SCALE

AMBULANCE DU 4ᵐᵉ CORPS

3ᴰ

Light caisson, normally drawn by 4 horse team. This vehicle is shown as a medical supply wagon.

Heavy wagons

The heavy wagons employed were merely supply wagons with a rounded canvas top supported on iron hoops. There were, of course, many variations on this theme.

Light wagons

Many modifications were made by the *ouvriers* of the Train, particularly in Spain where the French *Service de Sante* aroused much envy in the British. The light caisson shown carried medical supplies including stretchers, mattresses, a case of surgical instruments, lint, linen bandages and medicine.

The colour of the ambulances varied from a reddish brown to olive green. Those used by the Guard were all of the latter shade.

Mobile forge

Another interesting piece of equipment was the mobile forge which was widely used throughout the army. The one illustrated is a two wheel version, drawn by two horses, but a four-wheeled type, the front unit being the universal limber, was also used drawn by four horses.

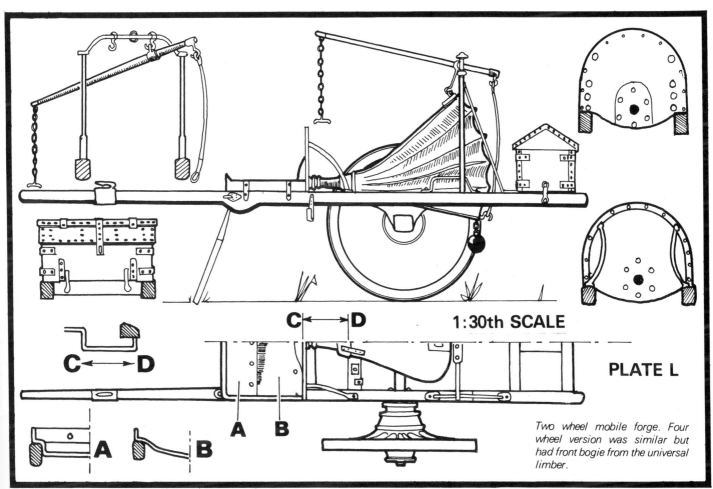

1:30th SCALE

PLATE L

Two wheel mobile forge. Four wheel version was similar but had front bogie from the universal limber.

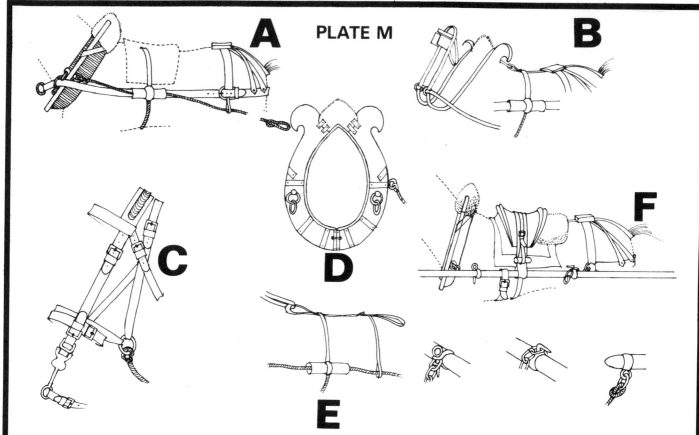

Details of draught horse harness. (A) Rear horse of team. left side, driven. (B) Bridle of right hand, rear horse. Otherwise identical with A. (C) Bridle of driven horse. Lead rope could be replaced by a leather rein and attached at a ring on the side of the halter. (D) Front view of halter. (E) Harness for lead horse. Identical each side except that the left hand horse was driven and carried a saddle. (F) Details of harness for shaft horse (eg, on wagon or light ambulance). Rear horse shown, lead horse harness as E.

Draught horse harness

Either a four or a six horse team harnessed in pairs could be used to pull guns or caissons. It would appear that six were generally used, especially for the horse artillery and for the 12 pdrs of the foot artillery. However, four horse teams are often seen in many contemporary prints and one would assume that either would be correct depending on the load to be hauled, the availability of horses etc.

The wooden halter used by the French was padded with black leather and had a small piece of sheepskin, either black or white, at the top. The wood was painted olive green and the straps were of buff leather. The metal rings, etc, were painted black. The harness itself was of buff coloured leather with the exception of the trace sheaths which were more usually a chestnut colour as were the saddles themselves. The blinkers were also buff coloured as was all the equipment on the riderless horses. On the driven horse, however, the guiding reins and bridle were of black leather. The two horses nearest the vehicle (in a four or six horse team) had chains running from a ring on the chest strap in the middle part of the halter to the limber pole. These were to enable the vehicle to be backed up which would be impossible with the rope traces.

The riderless horse had a single rein which was held by the rider opposite. The other, snaffle, reins went back over the halter and were held by a strap which went to the horses tail. A small rolled horse blanket, steel grey in colour, was tied to the top of the halter on a riderless horse and a small folded blanket was laid on the horses back.

PART 2: Organisation of Artillery Units

Horse Artillery of the Guard (Artillerie à Cheval de la Garde)

The *Artillerie à Cheval de la Garde* was formed as a regiment (by a decree of April 15, 1806) from the Light Artillery company which had been formed in the days of the Consular Guard. The Imperial Guard were the élite of the French army and in Napoleon's words: 'Nothing is too good for my Guard'. Consequently their uniforms and equipments were finer and more expensive than those of the Line Artillery. Rates of pay were also appreciably higher. When formed the regiment consisted of three squadrons, each composed of two companies.

Each company consisted of 25 Gunners 1st class, 25 Gunners 2nd class and 25 recruits. The remainder of the 97 men forming a company were officers and NCOs. In 1808 they were reduced to two squadrons each with two companies. In the latter part of 1813 a Young Guard company was formed.

Foot Artillery of the Guard (Artillerie à Pied de la Garde)

The *artillerie à Pied de la Garde* was created by a decree of April 12, 1808, and was composed of six companies of gunners and a company of *ouvriers-pontonniers* (Bridge-makers). Each company had four officers, a captain as commanding officer, another captain as second in command, and two lieutenants. There were

six NCOs consisting of a sergeant major (*Marechal des Logis Chef*), four sergeants (*Marechals des Logis*) and a farrier who ranked as a sergeant but only wore his stripe on the right sleeve. Seventy-eight men were formed from four corporals (*brigadiers*), four artificers, 20 gunners 1st class, 48 gunners and two drummers. The company of *ouvriers-pontonniers* had the same establishment of officers and NCOs as the artillery companies. The remaining men of the *ouvrier* company consisted of four *maitres Ouvriers Brigadiers* (craftsmen), 20 *ouvriers* 1st class, 24 *ouvriers*, 24 apprenctices and two drummers.

In June 1809 three companies of Young Guard or *Conscrit Artillerie* were formed. Eventually, by 1813, the Foot Artillery of the Guard consisted of six companies of Old Guard and sixteen companies of Young Guard.

During the Waterloo campaign there were six companies of Old Guard and a company of *ouvriers-pontonniers*. A Young Guard company was created but was not formed in time to participate in the campaign.

Horse Artillery of the Line (Artillerie à Cheval de Ligne)

The *Artillerie à Cheval de Ligne* consisted of six regiments from 1804 to 1810 and a seventh was created by a decree of 1810 to be formed from two companies of Dutch Horse Artillery. This was not found practicable, however, and the companies were absorbed by the 1st and 4th regiments. These regiments each consisted of six companies with a depot company in 1809 and in 1813 the 1st, 2nd and 3rd Regiments each had a seventh company. However, a situation report on the 5th Regiment in the Historical Archives of Vincennes gives an effectiveness of 721 men formed into eight companies varying between 79 and 132 men. Included in each company were 24 Gunners 1st class, four metal workers, four carpenters and two trumpeters. Each company had a battery of six 4 pdrs or four 4 pdrs and two 6 inch howitzers.

Foot Artillery of the Line
(Artillerie à Pied de Ligne)

The *artillerie à Pied de Ligne* consisted of eight regiments in 1804. In 1810 the regiment of Foot Artillery of the Dutch Army was incorporated making nine regiments. Each regiment consisted of 22 companies in 1804 rising to 28 in 1813.

Artillery Train of the Guard
(Train d'Artillerie de la Garde)

The *Train d'Artillerie de la garde* was formed as a battalion from the *Train d'Artillerie de Garde des Consuls*, and consisted of six companies. In 1807 there were two battalions, each of twelve companies.

The train was formed as a regiment in February 1813, and consisted of three battalions each of four companies and in April a second Regiment was formed. During the 100 days (Waterloo) a squadron of nine companies, plus one company of Young Guard, existed.

A company consisted of about 80 to 90 men with two officers, a sergeant major, two sergeants and four *brigadiers* and a trumpeter.

Artillery Train of the Line
(Train d'Artillerie de Ligne)

The *Train d'Artillerie de Ligne* consisted of ten battalions in 1804, each composed of 76 men. There were eleven in 1805 and thirteen in 1808. In 1810 a fourteenth was raised from the Dutch

army. During times of war an auxiliary battalion was raised and was distinguished by the word *bis* meaning literally 'twice' or 'again'. Hence 9th Battalion *Bis*.

(Bataillon d'Ouvriers d'Administration)

The *Train des Equipages* was formed to replace civilian workmen and drivers and in 1812 there were 22, the 18th being in charge of ambulances. In 1807 a battalion consisted of HQ staff and four companies. Each company was commanded by a *sous-lieutenant* with a *Marechal des Logis Chef* as second in command. There were two *Marechals des Logis*, four *brigadiers*, a trumpeter, a harness maker, two smiths, a wheelwright and 80 men. The harness maker, smiths and wheelwright rode in their wagons and were not individually mounted. Of the 93 men, nine rode normal saddle horses (ie, the officer and NCOs) and there were around 152 work horses pulling 34 wagons, an artillery park wagon, and a mobile forge.

Work Battalion
Equipment Train (Train des Equipages)

Brief mention must also be made here of the *Bataillon d'Ouvriers d'Administration* or work battalion. This, part of the Guard, consisted of companies in charge of the bakery, meat, forge and the field hospital. The soldiers wore steel grey short *habit veste* piped scarlet with scarlet pointed lapels and scarlet turnbacks. Waistcoats and trousers were steel grey, and fawn overcoats were worn. Their shakos were black with orange lace on the top band and orange plaited cords. A brass eagle plate was worn. Buttons were also brass. Originally when formed in 1812 scarlet carrot shaped pom pons were worn but in 1813 they wore scarlet plumes. The sergeants and sergeant majors had their shakos trimmed with mixed gold and scarlet lace and cords. Short muskets, bayonets and sabre briquets were carried.

Guard Equipment Battalion (Bataillon du Train des Equipages de la Garde)

In the same year (1812) a *Bataillon du Train des Equipages de la Garde* was formed. This unit provided vehicles for the whole Guard and was divided as follows. First company was responsible for the baggage, papers and forges of the different Corps of the Guard, the second company was in charge of the Field Hospital wagons, while the third took charge of all provision wagons. At that time there were 17 officers and 800 men. They had over 270 wagons and more than 1,200 horses. Their uniform was the same as the Line troops but with a scarlet piping to the collar, cuffs, lapels, turnbacks and pockets. Men on foot wore gaiters, and drivers wore skin breeches and high boots. Their pouch carried a crowned 'N' in white metal on the flap.

Their wagons were all painted dark green with the inscription: 'Garde Imperiale. Bataillon des Equipages. Campagnie No –.', in white on the lower sides.

PART 3: Artillery Uniforms

Horse Artillery of the Guard (Artillerie à Cheval de la Garde)

The dress of the Guard Horse Artillery was patterned on that of the Hussars consisting of an Imperial blue dolman laced across the front with 18 rows of scarlet braid and three vertical rows of brass buttons. This is shown in Plate P1.

Enlisted Mens' dress

The front edge and bottom of the dolman was laced scarlet as were the back seams and scarlet decorations appeared on the dolman sides below the arms as can be seen in the colour plate. An Imperial blue pelisse was carried (Plate P1) again with scarlet braiding and lace, and with black fur edging to the collar, front, bottom and cuffs. The pelisse, when worn, was fastened by loops on the left hand side over the buttons on the right. Therefore, there were two rows of buttons on the right side and only one on the left. (The dolman was the same but was fastened with buttonholes on the left side). The sash was scarlet with yellow bans, but otherwise similar to the Line Horse Artillery sash in Plate P2. For full dress were Hungarian breeches were worn, of Imperial blue, with ornate scarlet Hungarian knots at the front and a scarlet stripe on each side, looping at the seat.

Headgear was a black fur colpack with brass chin scales and a scarlet 'bag' hanging over the right rear as shown in Plate P1. On the left side a domed cockade supported a scarlet plume, and two scarlet flounders hung from the cockade. Scarlet plaited cords were sometimes worn in early years but appear to have been discontinued by 1808. The tricolour cockade carried a brass 'N' on the central blue portion.

A white Hungarian swordbelt was fastened by a brass 'S' clasp and the sabre and sabretache hung from three brass rings set into the belt on the left side. (See Plate P). The sabre was of light cavalry patterns with a brass scabbard and hilt. A black leather insert appeared between the carrying rings. The sword knot was white with a scarlet knot and tassell. The sabretache was of black leather with a blue cloth face bordered by a scarlet stripe.

From 1805-1810 the face of the sabretache was decorated by an eagle surmounted by a large crown. Beneath the eagle, crossed cannons appeared. All the decorations were gold with gold and green leaves rising from the cannon mouths. From 1810 to 1814 a simpler design consisting of a brass crowned eagle over crossed cannon was carried (Plate P1). From around 1809 a plain black leather sabretache was carried on the march. The brass eagle and cannon appeared on the face. A white belt, with stitched edges supported the pouch which was of black leather with a brass crowned eagle and cannon stamped on the flap. This shoulder belt fastened by a brass buckle on the rear left shoulder (see Plate P).

ARTILLERIE À CHEVAL DE LA GARDE: *(1) Gunner in summer dress without pelisse. (2) Gunner, Tenue de Campaign, 1812-14. (3) Marechal des Logis Chef (Sergeant Major) in riding coat; this coat was plain blue with brass button; the trefoil was gold on a scarlet patch; aiguillettes were gold and scarlet. The bicorne had a gold cockade strap with gold stiffeners and tassels; plume was scarlet and the Hungarian belt was white. (4) Gunner in Tenue de Route. (5) Brigadier (Corporal) in full dress with pelisse and sabretache.*

In *tenue de campaign* blue *pantalons à cheval* with black leather inserts and bottoms were worn. A scarlet stripe appeared on each side on which were 18 brass buttons. In *tenue de marche* no bag, plumes, cockade or flounders were worn. A scarlet cord trefoil shoulder strap was worn on the left shoulder to keep the pouch belt in place. This trefoil was much smaller than the usual type of trefoil. For service dress a long tailed *habit coat* was worn with pointed lapels. The coat was Imperial blue with scarlet turnbacks, pointed cuffs, and piping, as shown in Plate P2. A scarlet trefoil shoulder strap was worn on the right shoulder and a scarlet aiguillette on the left. Blue cloth grenades decorated the turnbacks. A scarlet braided waistcoat with three rows of buttons was worn, and the normal hungarian breeches. No sabretache was worn with the *habit coat*. The *habit coat* was also worn on the march with the *pantalons à cheval*, already described, and usually with a plain blue, straight bottomed, double-breasted waistcoat.

In *tenue de ville*, a *habit coat* was worn as described for service dress but with a black bicorne hat with scarlet tasselled pulls, stiffeners and plume. The cockade strap was also scarlet. The blue field service cap was of the usual pattern, piped and laced scarlet with a scarlet grenade at the front (see Plate P5). The greatcoat with a short cape was blue. Bicornes for NCOs (*Merechals*) had mixed gold and scarlet pulls and stiffeners and a gold lace cockade strap. The *Marechal des Logis Chef* had a mixed gold and scarlet sword knot and strap.

Trumpeters

Trumpeters were, as was usual with most Guard regiments, extremely colourful. In 1806 there were 18 trumpeters, a *Brigadier-Trompette* and a *Trompette-Major*. In 1808 when the regiment was reduced in size there were 8 trumpeters and a *Trompette-Major*; and in 1813, 12 trumpeters and a *Trompette-Major*.

The full dress uniform for Guard Horse Artillery trumpeters from 1804-1806 consisted of a rose-hued crimson (light crimson) pelisse, and dolman of sky blue with rose crimson cuffs. Breeches were sky blue. In 1806 the dolman became crimson, with sky blue cuffs, and the pelisse sky blue. Breeches remained the same. The trumpeter's dolman and pelisse (Plate P1) differed from the ordinary rank and file in that they had five rows of buttons. All braiding and lace was a mixture of gold and crimson except on the items which were rose crimson, then on these the braiding was gold and sky blue. Fur trim on the pelisse was black. The

shoulder belt and pouch was identical to the ordinary guardsman's. The barrel sash was sky blue with mixed gold and crimson barrels. Cords were mixed gold and crimson.

The sabretache was faced sky blue with a gold crowned eagle, and crossed cannon, and gold lace, shown in Plate P1. The full dress colpack was of white fur with a sky blue bag – piped gold and crimson, gold and crimson flounders, and a sky blue, tipped white plume. Brass chin scales were worn.

Service dress consisted of a sky blue *habit coat* with Imperial blue collar, lapels (pointed) and pointed cuffs. The collar, lapels, cuffs, turnbacks and pockets were piped crimson, inside which the collar, lapels and cuffs also carried a lace stripe of gold. The vest was braided with gold and crimson as were the breeches. Gold crossed cannon or grenades decorated the sky blue turnbacks. A gold trefoil on a crimson patch was worn on the right shoulder and a mixed gold and crimson aiguillette on the left.

Boots were trimmed with gold and crimson for both service and full dress. The service wear colpack was of black fur with a sky blue bag piped gold and crimson. Flounders were gold and crimson and the plume was sky blue, tipped white. Trumpet cords were gold and crimson.

In *tenue de route* sky blue *pantalons à cheval* were worn with black leather inserts and a crimson stripe each side with 18 brass buttons. A plain black leather sabretache identical to the mens' would normally be carried if the pelisse was worn on the march. No sabretache was worn with the *habit coat*.

Tenue de ville consisted of service dress with a black bicorne. The bicorne had mixed gold and sky blue pull tassels and stiffeners and the cockade strap was gold. The plume was again sky blue tipped white. *Brigadier Trompettes* wore two gold lace inverted chevrons on each arm, and *Trompette-Majors* wore three gold lace chevrons. The trumpeter's sword knot was white with the end and tassel of mixed gold and crimson.

Officers' dress

Officers wore the same style uniform as the men but with old lace and braid on the dolman, pelisse, breeches and boots (Plate P1). In common with the trumpeters. Officers wore five rows of buttons on the dolman and pelisse. The fur edging to the pelisse was grey. The colpack was of black fur and had a scarlet bag, piped gold. Flounders and plaited cords were also gold and the plume was scarlet. The breeches were ornamented by 'spear heads' in gold, the number of laces being indicative of rank. The sabretache was of red leather with a gold stripe and decoration as the men (Plate P1). A simplified sabretache for use on the march was of black leather, piped around the edge with gold and with a gold crowned eagle over crossed cannon and a small gold grenade beneath. The Hungarian sword belt was red, edged gold (see Plate Q). The shoulder belt was also red edged gold and the pouch was of red leather, edged in gold with a gilt eagle over crossed cannon. An alternative pouch belt was also of red leather, edged in gold with gold buttons and the usual belt decoration (ie, a gold *tete de medusa* with chains to a shield) was replaced by crossed cannon, surmounted by a crown. (See Plate P).

On the march a red leather cover, which buttoned down the centre with gold buttons, was usually worn over the pouch belt. In service dress the same pattern or *habit coat* was worn as for other ranks but with a gold full epaulette on the left shoulder and a gold aiguillette on the right. Turnback grenades were gold. The blue waistcoat was also braided gold.

Pantalons à cheval were identical to the men's, but as an alternative long tight blue trousers with gold stripes at the sides, separated by blue piping, could be worn. The sword knot was always completely gold. In *tenue de ville* or for social occasions the *habit coat* would be worn with a white instead of black neck stock, and a white waistcoat, white knee breeches, white stockings and black buckled shoes. A light epée was carried on a white waist belt with passed under the front flap to the breeches. A black bicorne with gold cockade strap, stiffeners and tassels with a scarlet plume was worn. In summer the carrying of a pelisse was not usual (this applied to all ranks).

ARTILLERIE À CHEVAL DE LA GARDE: *(1).Officer in Tenue de Campaign, 1806-7. (2) Officer, mounted, full dress.*

PLATE N

Horse Artillery cuff & arrowhead pantalon markings. **(1)** *Lieutenant.* **(2)** *Captain.* **(3)** *Chef d'Escadron.* **(4)** *Major & Colonel (centre stripe silver for a major).* **(5)** *Scarlet turnbacks on collars of some greatcoats of Artillerie à Pied de la Garde.* **(6)** *Early Horse Artillery shako with cockade detail on left side.* **(7)** *Early officers' pattern Horse Artillery shako.* **(8)** *Shako in protective oilskin cover for inclement weather.* **(9)** *Shako plate, Artillerie à Pied de Ligne 1807-10.* **(10)** *Shako plate, Train d'Artillerie de Ligne.* **(11)** *Pokalem, fatigue cap, dark blue piped scarlet.* **(12)** *Shako plate, Train d'Artillerie de la Garde.* **(13)** *Foot officer's gorget plate.* **(14)** *Shako plate, Guard Regiments.* **(15)** *Shako plate, Artillerie à Pied de Ligne. 1812-15.* **(16)** *NCO rank stripes for pointed & square cuffs, Corporal.* **(17)** *Sergeant.* **(18)** *Sergeant Major.* **(19)** *Detail of vertical lace of imperial livery. Yellow lace, black divisions, piped scarlet with dark green 'N's & eagles.* **(20)** *Button, Train d'Artillerie de Ligne.* **(21)** *Button, Artillerie à Pied de Ligne.* **(22)** *Button, Artillerie à Pied de la Garde.* **(23)** *Button, Train d'Artillerie de la Garde.*

10 5ᴱ Bⁿ. Tⁿ. D'ART.ᴿᴵᴱ

12 N

15 4

PLATE N

Horse furniture

Officers' horse furniture consisted of a blue shabraque piped scarlet with a gold lace stripe. Gold crowned eagles appeared in the rear corners. The valise was blue piped scarlet and laced gold. For full dress occasions a panther skin shabraque was used with a gold lace edge piped both sides of the gold with scarlet and with blue vandyking at the extreme edge (Plate P6). Red leather straps appeared on the panther skin, but otherwise all straps, etc were black. The exception was the snaffle rein and bridle which was gold and the stirrup leathers which were red.

The men's horse furniture also featured a blue shabraque with pointed rear ends, piped and trimmed scarlet. The cylindrical valise was blue, piped and laced scarlet. The snaffle rein and bridle were scarlet and the remaining straps and leatherwork were black with the exception of the stirrup leathers which were buff. On campaign or on the march a white skeepskin was used in place of the cloth shabraque, having scarlet vandyking at the edges (Plate P6).

A sky blue shabraque piped and laced scarlet with scarlet crowned eagles in the rear quarters was used on trumpeters horses. The cylindrical valise was sky blue, piped and laced scarlet (plate P1).

Dark bay horses were used by the Guard Artillery but in later years blacks were used when available. The trumpeters always rode greys.

Horse Artillery of the Line (Artillerie à Cheval de Ligne)

The Line Horse Artillery wore a uniform almost identical to the Guard but did not carry a pelisse. The dolman was Imperial blue with a blue collar and scarlet cuffs. The collar, front and bottom edges and rear seams were laced scarlet. Eighteen rows of scarlet braid decorated the front of the dolman with three rows of half round brass buttons. The sash was blue with red barrels and cords as in Plate P2. Hussar breeches and boots were worn, as for Guard artillery. Service dress consisted of a long tailed coat of dark blue, piped scarlet as shown in Plate P2.

Trumpeters' coats were in reversed colours compared to those of the men, and the precise style is shown in Plate P2.

In the 1810-12 period some regiments wore the so-called *Habit Kinski*. In 1812 the simpler *habit veste* was issued, having a plain blue collar and pointed scarlet cuffs. Turnbacks were scarlet with blue grenades and scarlet laced *soubisse* pockets. Lapels were piped scarlet and scarlet epaulettes were worn.

Pantalons à cheval were blue, with black leather inserts. Angled, three pointed pocket flaps appeared at the front, piped scarlet, and there was a scarlet stripe on each outer seam with 18 brass buttons riding on it. Alternatively blue cloth covered buttons with scarlet piping to the rear of the button were used. Sabretaches were of brown leather with a scarlet lace border and face of blue cloth, with laurel device and scarlet regimental number, plus either a gold crown or a small circlet of laurel leaves above (Plate P2). Alternatively a brass number over brass crossed cannon with a brass grenade below was worn (Plate P2).

The Hungarian sword belt was white and a brass hilted light cavalry sabre was carried in a brass or steel scabbard. The sword knot was white. The original shako issued in 1805 was very simple without plate or chin scales. It was not bell shaped as were the later issues, but cylindrical. The cockade was held in place by a scarlet cord strap and simple scarlet cords were carried, with a scarlet plume appearing at the front. The usual shako was worn from 1806. The plume was scarlet and scarlet flounders hung on the right side. Sometimes the top and bottom bands were scarlet (Plate P2).

The new regulations of 1812 provided for a shako with top and botton braids in scarlet and scarlet chevrons. The plate took the form of an eagle over a semicircular shield, upon which appeared crossed cannon surmounted by a grenade over a white metal number (see Plate N). Either a scarlet plume or a scarlet pom-pon was carried.

The Line Horse Artillery greatcoat was dark blue, single breasted and with a short cape. The pouch belt was white and the pouch was made of black leather with brass crossed cannons (see Plate P). No carbine was carried by the Horse Artillery.

Trumpeters

For service dress, the *habit coat* was worn in scarlet cloth, with collar, pointed cuffs and turnbacks of blue. The pointed shoulder straps and pointed lapels were piped blue and the tops of the lapels were rounded while the collar and cuffs had gold lacing. The braided vest and breeches were blue laced scarlet.

There were several variations on the standard uniform. For example a trumpeter of the 3rd Regiment is shown by the artist Knotel to be wearing the standard uniform already described but with a colpack of black fur with a plain scarlet 'bag' and a scarlet plume instead of a shako. Another variation was for the Hussar uniform already described to be worn but with breeches of scarlet laced blue. The shako was worn in this instance.

The 2nd Regiment is shown in contemporary prints in service dress, as described, but with a scarlet pom-pon on the shako with a black plume and a scarlet tip.

Perhaps the most colourful and unusual variation in contemporary prints shows a *Trompette-Major*, regiment unknown, who wears a scarlet *habit coat* and breeches with a blue waistcoat. The coat has blue pointed lapels with rounded tops, collar and cuffs. The collar is laced gold and piped scarlet. The cuffs, however, are shown piped white and the full epaulettes and the turnbacks are also shown white. Red grenades decorated the turnbacks (as they did in the case of blue turnbacks). The lapels were piped scarlet and the blue waistcoat was braided and edged scarlet. A whitened leather waist belt was worn with a brass plate. The breeches had blue 'spearhead' decorations, not Hungarian knots as was usual, and the breeches had a blue stripe on the seams. A gold lace chevron appeared above the cuff and the trumpet cord was scarlet. The headgear was most unusual, not by virtue of the fact that it was a lancers *czapska*, which was often worn by musicians, but because the 'sunray' plate at the front had a brass centre and silver rays. The top part was blue, piped scarlet with a gold lace centre bank and a black turban. Chin scales were of brass and the black peak was trimmed with white metal. The plume rose from a yellow pom-pon and had a blue lower half and a scarlet top half.

A trumpeter of the 2nd Regiment in Spain is described as wearing the dolman of blue (as worn by the troops) with blue cuffs laced scarlet to form an Austrian knot at the point. The sash was scarlet with blue barrels. A pelisse was carried, in blue with scarlet lacing, and *pantalons à cheval* were blue with a scarlet stripe bearing brass buttons. A black colpack was worn without a plume or 'bag'. Trumpeters always had grey horses.

Imperial livery

In 1812 the Imperial livery was introduced which served to standardise the dress of the trumpeter.

The coat was green with the collar blue. The cuffs and turnbacks were scarlet as was the soubisse piping on the rear pockets. Scarlet epaulettes were worn with a green retaining strap. The collar, cuffs and turnbacks were laced with Imperial

ARTILLERIE À CHEVAL DE LIGNE: *(1) Cannonier, 1810, in Habit Kinski and Pantalons à Cheval. (2) cannonier, 1812, in Habit Veste.*

livery. The chest had double stripes of livery across the 1st, 3rd, 5th, 7th and 9th buttons. Blue grenades were worn on the turnbacks. Breeches were blue with scarlet 'spearheads' and stripes. Boots were plain, without piping. The trumpet cord was mixed yellow and green. The shako was without cords or lace and a scarlet pom-pon only was worn although the plume was probably retained for full dress appearances.

Officers' uniforms

Officers of the Line Horse Artillery wore a variety of uniform types, no doubt because the regiments were spread out by batteries over a wide area, thereby giving the Captains and Lieutenants in command, a great deal of autonomy.

In general the hussar type uniform of the men was worn but with all lacing, braiding and buttons in gold. The lacings on the chest of the dolman numbered eighteen and had five vertical rows of buttons. The cuffs were scarlet with gold lacing. This lacing formed the first of the rank stripes which were worn on the cuffs.

The waist sash was blue with gold barrels and cords. A pelisse was often worn by officers of the Line Horse Artillery and it was blue with gold braid and lace. Identical rank stripes to those on the dolman were carried on the cuffs and the pelisse was bordered with grey or fawn fur.

Hussar style breeches were worn with gold stripes, and gold lace 'spearheads' on the front indicated rank (see Plate P2 and N).

A service uniform consisted of a *habit coat* with long tails. The coat was blue with scarlet pointed cuffs and scarlet turnbacks. The pointed lapels were rounded at the top and piped scarlet as were the soubise pockets. The collar was plain blue without piping. The turnback grenades and buttons were gold. A full epaulette was worn on the left shoulder and a contra-epaulette on the right. Senior lieutenants had a stripe of scarlet along the strap part while junior lieutenants had a scarlet lozenge.

In 1813 the *Habit kinski* and the short *habit veste* were worn.

The *Habit Kinski* had scarlet piping with scarlet turnbacks while the *habit veste* had a plain collar with scarlet piping on the lapel edges and the soubisse pockets. In both cases the pointed cuffs were scarlet and gold grenades appeared on the turnbacks. Epaulettes were worn although it would appear that the contra-epaulette was not always worn on the *Habit Kinski*.

In *tenue de ville* a blue surtout, piped scarlet at the front and bottom and with scarlet turnbacks and pointed cuffs was worn.

Epaulettes were carried and again it is possible that the contra epaulette was not worn. A white waistcoat just showed beneath the surtout and yellow skin breeches were worn with white stockings and black shoes with silver buckles. The bicorne was worn but usually without a plume.

Officers' head-dress

At the beginning of the Empire the shako of Line Horse Artillery officers had cords, flounders and the top band of gold. A large gold lace cockade strap secured the tri-colour cockade to the front and no shako plate was carried. Two gold lace chevrons were worn on the sides of the shako with the point of the 'V' to the top. (See Plate N). Later the taller bell-shaped shako was worn with the addition of the eagle plate (as worn by the men) and with brass chin straps. Other details were the same but the chevrons disappeared. Senior officers had two laces of gold braid at the top of the shako, the lower one half the width of the upper and distinctly separate from each other. A scarlet plume without a pom-pon was worn in both cases. For senior officers a white plume was worn (Plate P4). The black fur colpack was also worn by many officers with a scarlet 'bag' piped gold, with a gold tassel and a scarlet plume at the front. Beneath the dolman or the pelisse if worn (rather than slung over the shoulder) and also beneath the *habit coat* a blue, sometimes scarlet waistcoat was worn braided with gold lace and with three rows of buttons; The edges were also laced gold.

On campaign or on the march the shako was worn without cords and the colpack without the 'bag'. In place of the plume on the shako a scarlet pom-pon with a gold tuft was usually carried. No plume at all was fitted on the colpack. During the early campaign most officers would appear to have worn a black bicorne with a gold cockade strap and gold tassesls at the ends with a scarlet plume.

Accoutrements

The sabretache was carried when the dolman or pelisse were worn. It was of dark red leather with a blue cloth face bearing a gold numeral surrounded by gold laurel leaves and a gold circlet of leaves above the number. A gold stripe edged the blue cloth.

The Hungarian sword belt and sabretache straps were usually of red leather edged with gold although black edged gold was also worn (see Plate P). A plain black leather belt was also sometimes used with the *habit coat*.

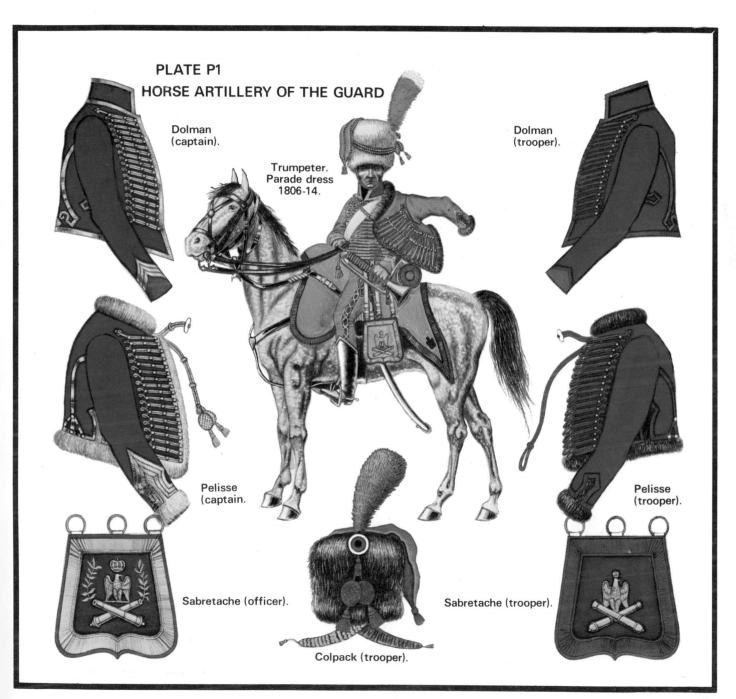

PLATE P1

HORSE ARTILLERY OF THE GUARD

Dolman (captain).

Dolman (trooper).

Trumpeter. Parade dress 1806-14.

Pelisse (captain.

Pelisse (trooper).

Sabretache (officer).

Colpack (trooper).

Sabretache (trooper).

ARTILLERIE À CHEVAL DE LIGNE: *(1) Officer, Tenue de Route. Pantalons were grey with a single scarlet stripe; note unusual sabretache with black fur. (2) Officer, Tenue de Ville. Note epaulette on left shoulder and no contra-epaulette. (3) Officer in cloak; lower edge of cape trimmed in gold lace. (4) Trumpeter in coat; note rounded tops to lapels. (5) Trumpet-Major in czapska.*

The pouch was of red leather with gold lace around the edge of the flap and crossed cannon surmounted by either a grenade or the regimental number in yellow brass on the centre (see Plate P). The pouch belt was also of red leather edged gold, usually with gold buttons running down the centre line. A lion's head in gold was featured on the belt with two gold chains looping to a gold shield worn lower down.

The officer's riding coat was blue with a short cape around the shoulders, the bottom edge of which was laced with gold. A double breasted riding coat was also worn with gold buttons and also with a short cape the lower edge of which was again laced gold. The pouch and belt and the Hungarian sword belt without sabretache were all worn outside the riding coat.

Horse furniture

Horse furniture for officers consisted for full dress of a blue shabraque with pointed rear ends, laced gold and piped blue. The saddle was covered by a panther skin which was vandyked gold. The surcingle and the retaining straps were brown. Bronze stirrups with red leather straps were carried. The bridle and reins were of black leather, the snaffle bridle resting on scarlet cloth which showed at the edges. Saddle details for a Line Horse Artillery officer are shown in Plate P2. A gold grenade or regimental number sometimes appeared in the rear quarters but more often than not it was plain blue. For normal service the panther skin was not carried.

Horse furniture for enlisted men consisted of a white sheepskin edged with scarlet vandyking, and a cylindrical valise of dark blue laced scarlet at the ends. The valise had either plain centres or a white number denoting the regiment (Plate P6). Stirrup leathers were buff and the remaining horse strappings were black. Horse furniture for trumpeters featured a black sheepskin, vandyked scarlet and with a blue valise laced scarlet. Either a grenade or the regimental number appeared at the valise ends.

Swords

Light cavalry style swords were carried on all occasions except in *tenue de ville* when a straight epée with a gilt hilt and gold sword knot was carried in a black leather scabbard suspended from a white waist belt. The light cavalry scabbards were either all brass or steel though sometimes a black leather scabbard ornamented with brass was used. The hilt was gilt and the sword knot gold (see Plate Q).

Foot Artillery of the Guard (Artillerie à Pied de la Garde)

When the foot regiment of the Guard was formed in 1808 the uniform differed but little from that of the Line regiments. Only better quality cloth, the eagle plates on the shako, the pouch ornament, buttons, and the stitched edges to the belts served to distinguish them. Also, at first, distinctive red epaulettes were worn but these were subsequently adopted by most Line regiments. It was not until May, 1810 that the characteristic bearskin with its visor was adopted (Plate P3).

Enlisted Men's uniform

A normal long tailed cost of Imperial blue with square lapels and cuffs with three pointed slashes was worn as shown in Plate P3. The cuffs and turnbacks were scarlet, the latter decorated with blue cloth grenades (or gold braid grenades for NCOs). The garment was trimmed with scarlet piping and buttons were brass. From the formation of the regiment until 1810 the collar was plain blue but from that time the collar was piped scarlet and the cuff slashes became wholly scarlet (plate P3). The waistcoat was plain blue though it is possible that during the summer months it was replaced by a white one for parade war. Breeches were plain blue. The field service cap (*Bonnet de police*) was dark blue, laced and piped scarlet with a scarlet grenade at the front.

At first the overcoat was dark blue but during 1811 was replaced progressively by a new coat of a mixture of dark blue and white thread. This blue-grey colour was known as 'Steel Grey' and was virtually forced on the French by the shortage of indigo dye. The greatcoat fastened by brass buttons down the front. The collar and cuffs were piped scarlet and in early years at least a scarlet shaped patch appeared on each side of the collar at the front (see Plate N). Scarlet epaulettes were normally worn on the greatcoat. Long blue trousers were worn on the march, either over or tucked into short black gaiters to below the knee.

A long sleeved blue waistcoat which buttoned down the front with seven brass buttons, was straight cut at the bottom, had single brass buttons on the cuffs and plain blue shoulder straps, was worn with long blue trousers and the service cap for fatigue duties.

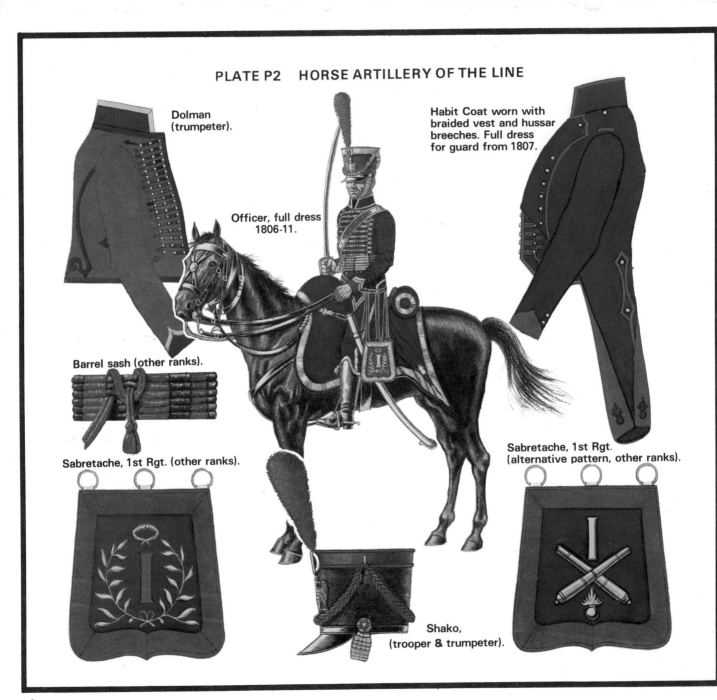

PLATE P2   HORSE ARTILLERY OF THE LINE

Dolman (trumpeter).

Officer, full dress 1806-11.

Habit Coat worn with braided vest and hussar breeches. Full dress for guard from 1807.

Barrel sash (other ranks).

Sabretache, 1st Rgt. (other ranks).

Sabretache, 1st Rgt. (alternative pattern, other ranks).

Shako, (trooper & trumpeter).

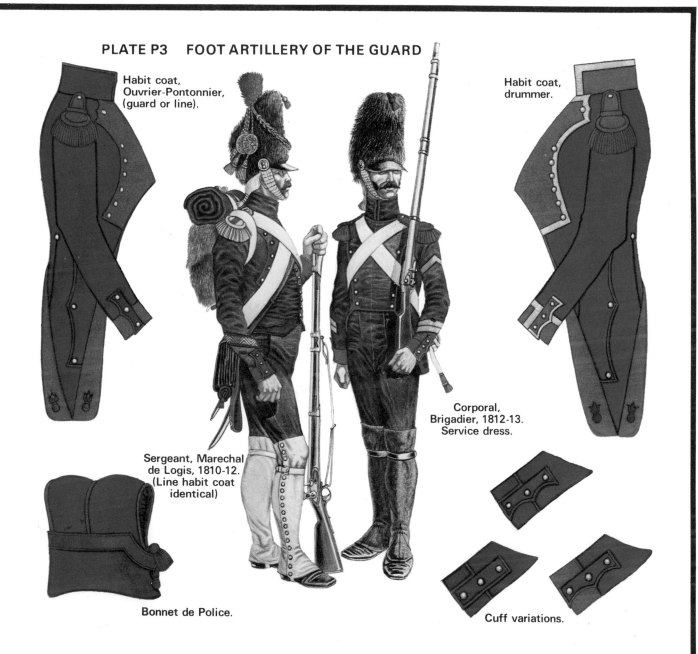

PLATE P3   FOOT ARTILLERY OF THE GUARD

Habit coat,
Ouvrier-Pontonnier,
(guard or line).

Habit coat,
drummer.

Sergeant, Marechal
de Logis, 1810-12.
(Line habit coat
identical)

Corporal,
Brigadier, 1812-13.
Service dress.

Bonnet de Police.

Cuff variations.

Head wear

Until 1810 a black shako was worn. The top band was scarlet as were the plaited cords and plume. The brass plate showed a crowned eagle over crossed cannons and the chin strap was of brass. On the march, etc, a black oilskin cover was worn and the plume was replaced by a scarlet pom-pon.

In 1810 the bearskin with a plain black leather peak was distributed to the gunners and *ouvriers* and this is shown in Plate P3. From 1811 the original chin strap on the bearskin was replaced by brass chin scales. On the march no cords, patch or plume were worn and from 1813 flounders were rarely worn. *Ouvriers-pontonniers* wore the same uniform as the gunners but additionally had scarlet lapels (Plate P3).

Tenue de ville

In *tenue de ville* the normal coat was worn with a white waistcoat and white breeches in white stockings and buckled shoes. A black bicorne with a scarlet cockade strap and scarlet tassels replaced the shako or bearskin. The sabre briquet was carried on the shoulder strap.

Drummers

Drummers wore the same uniform as the artillerymen but with scarlet collar, lapels, cuffs and cuff slashes, all with gold lace edging (Plate P3). The drum carriage was of whitened leather with a white apron. Drum was mid blue with brass rims and white cord tensioners. Brass grenades appeared between the tensioners. The Drum Major in 1808-11 wore the same uniform as a drummer but with gold epaulettes and high leather boots. The waistcoat was laced gold at the edges. Two gold lace stripes appeared above each cuff. He wore a black bicorne, laced at the edge with gold and which had gold tassels and a gold cockade strap. A bunch of feathers, two red and one sky blue, was attached over the cockade with a white plume rising from them. Black gauntlets were worn, also trimmed with gold lace.

Sappers

A *sapeur* around 1808 wore the same uniform as the gunners but headwear was a black colpack with a scarlet bag piped gold, and a scarlet plume. Red crossed axes with a red grenade above them were worn on the upper arms. Crossed brass axes appeared on the belt which carried the axe holder. A white apron reached below kness under the coat and a white waist belt with brass square plate was worn over the apron. The axe had a black wooden handle with a brass ferrule at the end. The blade was of steel.

Accoutrements

Gunners and *ouvriers* carried a sabre briquet and bayonet on a whitened buff leather shoulder belt over the right shoulder. The hilt of the short sabre was brass and the scabbard black, as was the bayonet scabbard. Both were heeled in brass. The sword knot was white with a scarlet tassel. A cartridge pouch was carried on a belt over the left shoulder and was of black leather, the flap being embossed with a brass crowned eagle over crossed cannon (see Plate P). On the march a black oilskin cover could be worn over the flap. The field service cap was carried rolled on straps under the flap. A hide pack was carried on the back, usually reddish-fawn, sometimes with white patches. The edges were sometimes whitened and the rolled greatcoat was carried on top of the pack, fastened by a white strap. Gaiters were black with brass buttons for normal wear and white with white cloth covered buttons for parades.

PLATE P

(1) Cowhide knapsack with greatcoat rolled on top. Used by foot artillery. **(2)** Foot artillery cartridge box. **(3)** Cylindrical valise. **(4)** Square portmanteau. **(5)** Carbine sling, worn over pouch belt by horse artillerymen. **(6)** Cartridge pouch belt for horse artillerymen. **(7)** Primer tube pouch with primer pin attached to flap. carried by 'No. 5' of gun crew. **(8)** 'English' saddle, often adopted by line horse artillery officers. **(9)** Hungarian sword belt clasp. Officers pattern. **(10)** As 9, for enlisted men. **(11)** Detail of Hungarian sword belt. Officers pattern. **(12)** Enlisted men's pattern Hungarian sword belt for horse artillery, showing sabre & sabretache slings. **(13)** Canvas waistbelt for bandages. Worn by 'infirmier'. **(14)** Sabre briquet & bayonet belt, carried by foot artillerymen. **(15)** Officers cartridge pouch belts (red leather with gold trim) for horse artillery. **(16)** Officers pouch. Artillerie à Cheval de la Garde in red leather with gold lace trim. **(17)** Trumpeters & enlisted men's pouch. Artillerie à Cheval de la Garde. Black leather with a brass eagle. **(18)** Cartridge box, Artillerie à Pied de la Garde. Black leather with a brass plate. **(19)** Cartridge box. Artillerie à Pied de Ligne. Black leather, brass cannons. **(20)** Enlisted man's pouch, Artillerie à Cheval de Ligne. Black leather brass cannons. **(21 & 22)** Officers pouch. Artillerie à Cheval de Ligne. Red leather with gold lace.

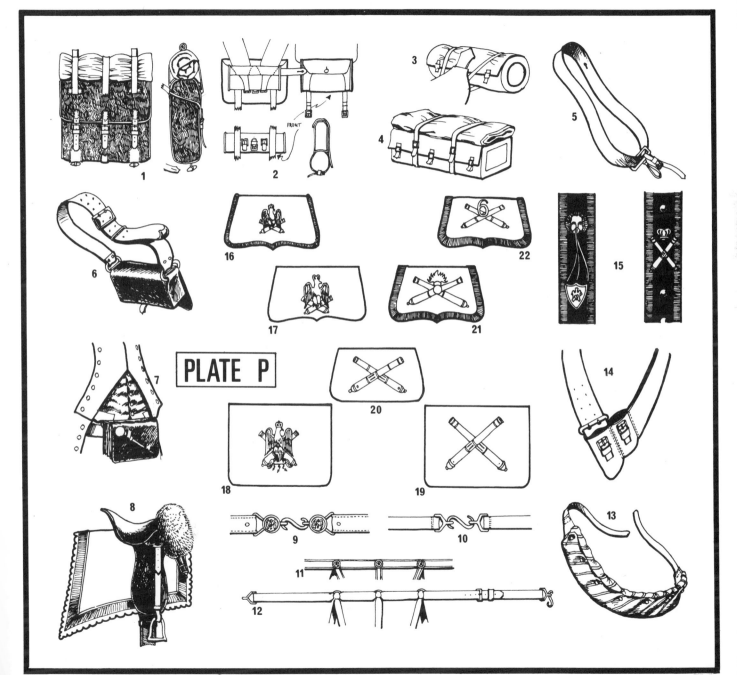

PLATE P

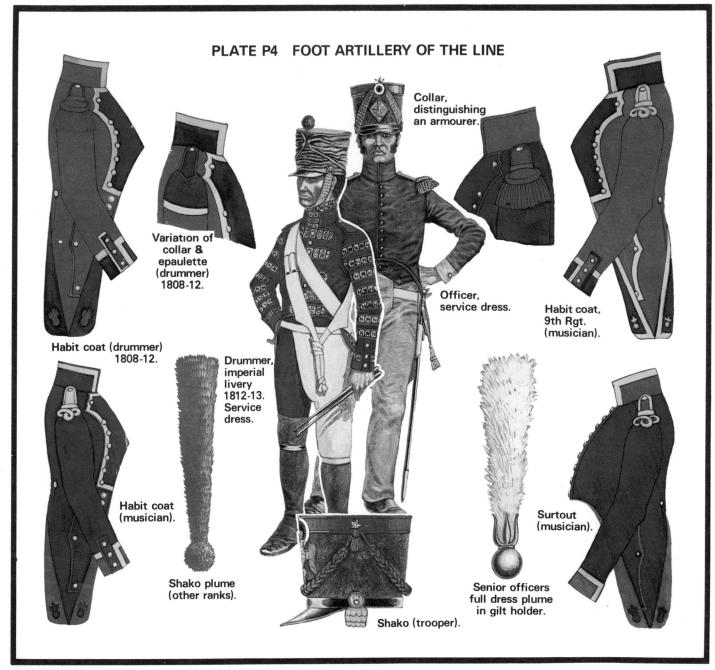

PLATE P4 FOOT ARTILLERY OF THE LINE

Variation of collar & epaulette (drummer) 1808-12.

Habit coat (drummer) 1808-12.

Habit coat (musician).

Shako plume (other ranks).

Drummer, imperial livery 1812-13. Service dress.

Collar, distinguishing an armourer.

Officer, service dress.

Habit coat, 9th Rgt. (musician).

Surtout (musician).

Senior officers full dress plume in gilt holder.

Shako (trooper).

PLATE P5
ARTILLERY TRAIN OF THE LINE & GUARD

Soldier in 'Habit Kinski',
service dress
1810-11.

Soldier, 1812-15.
Full dress.

Habit coat
with braided
waistcoat
(sergeant).

Habit veste, 1810-11.

Full dress shako 1813-14 (other ranks).

Bonnet de Police,
(guard, other ranks).

33

Officers' dress

Officers of the Guard Foot Artillery wore a gold epaulette on the left shoulder and a contra epaulette on the right. Turnback grenade badges were gold as was the top band of the shako and the cords of the shako and bearskin. The scarlet plume on the shako was carried in a gilt tulip shaped holder. The commanding officer of a battalion also wore a gold aiguilette on the right shoulder with the contra epaulette, and the plume was white tipped scarlet. A gilt gorget plate was worn by all officers except when the *surtout* was worn. This was a single breasted coat, fastened at the front by nine brass buttons and is shown in Plate P4. Turnbacks and all piping were scarlet with gold grenades and the gold epaulette and contra epaulette was worn.

On foot the sword was carried on a white leather shoulder belt but on horseback a black waistbelt with a gilt square plate was used. Senior officers wore black gauntlet gloves, trimmed with gold lace.

Officers' horse furniture

Horse furniture for mounted officers of the Guard Foot Artillery is shown. The saddle itself was of white or fawn leather. The cloth was piped blue and had two stripes of gold lace, the inner being half the width of the outer. Double holster hoods carried the same facing as the saddle cloth and the rubbing plates were of black leather. The tips of the holsters, just visible below the hoods, were gilt. Girth was also gold. The stirrup leather was red and the snaffle rein and bridle gold. All other horse gear was black.

Young Guard

Young Guard companies *only* wore the shako, otherwise they were identical to the Old Guard. Young Guard officers were permitted to wear the bearskin.

Foot Artillery of the Line
(Artillerie à Pied de Ligne)

This corps had an almost identical uniform to that of the Foot Artillery of the Guard. Dark blue was again the predominant colour with the collar, cuffs and square lapels were piped scarlet.

The turnbacks were scarlet ornamented with blue grenades. The cuff flaps were either all scarlet or blue piped scarlet. Pointed shoulder straps were specified in the orders concerning the Line Artilley uniform and these were blue, piped scarlet. However, in practice from around 1811, it was common to find fringed epaulettes of scarlet being worn by the Line Artillery. Also the cuffs from around 1807 began to appear scarlet, with blue cuff slashes piped scarlet.

The regulations of 1812 introduced the *habit veste* with short tails. Again the collar, edges of the lapels, shoulder straps (or scarlet epaulettes), and three-pointed vertical pockets were piped scarlet. Blue cloth grenades appeared on the scarlet turnbacks. We must note, however, that in many instances piping was omitted from the collar of the *habit veste*. Buttons in all cases were of brass.

Blue breeches were worn with black gaiters for service or winter wear and white gaiters with summer or full dress wear. In 1812, short black gaiters were introduced coming to the top of the calves. On campaign or on the march long blue trousers were worn from about 1808, and white or black gaiters were worn beneath the trousers. A contemporary illustration also shows mid-brown trousers around 1810-12 and this is probably a case where local cloth had been used to replace worn items. In 1813 the long blue trousers could be seen with two scarlet stripes separated by blue piping. The waistcoats worn under the *habit coat* were usually dark blue with brass buttons and a 'V' cut out at the lower front. Many contemporary prints, however, show a square cut waistcoat piped down the front and along the bottom with scarlet.

Head wear

From 1804 to 1806 a black bicorne hat was worn with an aurore cockade strap and a scarlet plume for full dress and a scarlet carrot-shaped pom-pon for service dress. In 1807 when the shako appeared, chinscales were not worn at first but appear to have been introduced in 1808. The shako originally had scarlet lace on the top and bottom bands and a 'V' of scarlet lace at the sides. Sometimes, however, the 'V' did not appear (Plate P4). From 1811 the scarlet lace was rarely seen and the shako was entirely black. Scarlet plaited cords were worn, front and rear with scarlet flounders at the right side. These also seem to have disappeared around 1812. A multitude of pom-pon styles are shown in contemporary prints, either carrot shaped, round with a tuft, cylindrical with a tuft, flat disc shape, or a full plume rising from a round pom-pon. All were scarlet.

ARTILLERIE À PIED DE LA GARDE: *(1) Cannonier in Tenue d'Exercice. (2) Cannonier in Tenue de Route, 1808-10. (3) Cannonier in full dress, 1808-11. (4) Sapper. (4A) Red embroidered arm badge for sappers. (5) Cannonier in full dress, 1812-15, front and rear. (6) Cannonier in overcoat, 1812-14.*

PLATE P6 EQUIPMENT TRAIN HORSE FURNITURE

Soldier, 1812-13.
Service dress.

Driver, 1808-13.
Service dress.

Officer, full dress.
Horse Artillery of the Guard.

Gunner, Horse Artillery of the
Line. Service dress as for
Horse Artillery of the Guard.

Mounted Officer. Foot
Artillery of the Line.
Service dress.

Trumpeter, Artillery
Train of the Guard.

Soldier, Artillery Train
of the Guard.

Officer, Artillery Train
of the Line.

Soldier, Artillery Train
of the Line.

Saddle, with valise
for equipment train.

A variety of forms of shako plate appeared. From 1807 to 1810 the lozenge shaped plate was normal, stamped with a crowned eagle over crossed cannon with the regimental number below. Alternatively there was a crowned eagle on top of a rectangle or semi circular shield. In 1812, new regulations specified a crowned eagle on a semi circular shield which carried crossed cannon with a grenade above and a white metal number below. On either side of the eagle resting on top of the shield was a grenade. On campaign and on the march the shako was usually covered in a black oilskin cover.

Overcoats

The overcoat was dark blue and until around 1812 was single breasted with five cloth covered buttons. From that time the overcoat was double breasted with two rows of cloth covered buttons fastening to the right. The Line Artillery equipment followed that of the Guard with whitened leather pouch and sword belts. The pouch, of black leather, carried crossed brass cannon though from 1812 the flap was plain. All plates were brass (see Plate P).

The field service cap was of the usual pattern, of dark blue, piped scarlet with a scarlet tassel and on the front a cloth grenade of scarlet. In 1812 the 'Pokalem' service cap was introduced. This was a circular cap with flaps on the side which could be let down, covering the ears and neck and buttoned under the chin. This was also blue, piped scarlet with a scarlet regimental number at the front.

Other orders of dress

In *tenue de ville* the usual *habit coat* was worn, with a white waistcoat (in some cases double breasted) and off-white breeches, possibly of skin. The bicorne was worn and only the sabre was carried on its belt over the right shoulder. *Tenue d'exercice* (working dress) consisted of the field cap, a long sleeved blue waistcoat (with a white stock at the neck) buttoned down the front with ten buttons and with scarlet round cuffs. Blue breeches and black gaiters went with this.

Armourers were distinguished by their scarlet collar and cuffs with scarlet slashes also (Plate P4). *Ouvriers* had scarlet lapels, piped blue and scarlet cuffs and cuff slashes. Otherwise their uniform was as the normal artilleryman.

Musicians

Musicians wore the *habit coat* in most instances shown in Plate P4, of dark blue with blue waistcoat and breeches. Either turned down boots showing the fawn lining or hussar style boots were worn. The hussar boots had gold piping and tassels. A light epée was carried on a white shoulder strap over the right shoulder. The epée had a brass hilt and a gold sword knot and was carried in a black leather scabbard. The musicians' shako had a gold lace top band and scarlet plaited cords and flounders, but was otherwise the same as the rank and file s.

An exception to the above was the 9th Regiment whose musicians wore a scarlet coat with blue collar, lapels, cuffs and turnbacks in the style shown in Plate P4. At the rear waist buttons a *taille* was worn of gold lace (an inverted 'W') Gold grenades on scarlet patches were worn on the turnbacks. (The *taille*, and the scarlet patches, do not appear on the coloured illustration of this coat). Cuff slashes were scarlet piped blue (or, possibly gold). The headgear was in the form of the traditional lancers' *czapska* identical to that worn by the 2nd Lancers of the Imperial Guard with a scarlet top piped gold, gold lace centre strip and black turban. A gold plaited cord hung across the front from the sides of the cap top, and gold flounders hung at the right. A brass sunray plate with a white metal centre bearing a gilt crowned 'N' was worn at the front. The visor was black, edged with brass and chin scales were of brass. A white plume was worn above the cockade.

The Drum Major of this regiment wore an identical uniform with two gold lace stripes over each cuff and a cluster of three ostrich feathers, one blue, one white and one red on the *czapska* with a white plume rising from them. He also wore gold epaulettes.

A blue *surtout* with nine brass buttons fastening the front was also worn by musicians (Plate P4). In this case the collar was scarlet laced with gold as were the round cuffs. With this coat the epée was carried on a waist belt.

From 1804 to 1806, drummers wore the same uniform as the gunners with the addition of yellow or gold lace on the collar, lapels and on the scarlet cuffs, with all piping scarlet. The bicorne had scarlet stiffeners. In 1807 the drummers wore a scarlet coat with blue collar, lapels, cuffs and turnbacks. The collar, lapels and cuffs were laced yellow or gold with scarlet piping on the collar. Cuff slashes were scarlet, piped but in addition blue 'swallows nests' over the top of the sleeves laced at the bottom with yellow or gold lace, were worn (Plate P4). These 'swallows nests' were replaced by scarlet epaulettes and the collar also became scarlet. Cuff slashes became blue piped scarlet (Plate P4).

Finally in 1812 the drummers were uniformed in the Imperial livery as decreed by Napoleon (Plate P4 also see Plate N).

Drums were of brass with mid blue rims and white ropes. There is some doubt of the authenticity of a well-known illustration showing red rims but it is possible. The drum carriage and apron were of whitened leather and the drum sticks were of ebony with brass tipped handles.

Enlisted Men's side-arms

At first the Line artillery carried an unusual sabre briquet, which was issued in the time of the monarchy, having a brass hilt shaped in the form of an eagle's head with a brass cross bar. The blade widened toward the tip (see Plate Q). This unusual piece of equipment was, however, quickly replaced by the standard sabre briquet. In either case the sabre was carried in a black leather scabbard heeled with brass and the bayonet was in a brown leather scabbard. The sword knot was scarlet.

Officers' dress

Officers' uniforms followed the same pattern as the men's but with gold buttons and gold cords, plus a gold braid top band on the shako (Plate P4). Senior officers had two bands of gold lace. A gold contra epaulette was worn on the right shoulder and a gold epaulette on the left. Senior officers wore two gold epaulettes and turnback grenades were also gold.

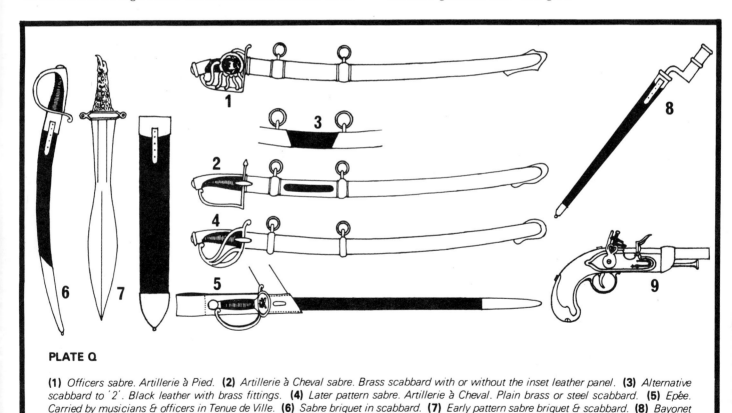

PLATE Q

(1) *Officers sabre. Artillerie à Pied.* **(2)** *Artillerie à Cheval sabre. Brass scabbard with or without the inset leather panel.* **(3)** *Alternative scabbard to '2'. Black leather with brass fittings.* **(4)** *Later pattern sabre. Artillerie à Cheval. Plain brass or steel scabbard.* **(5)** *Epée. Carried by musicians & officers in Tenue de Ville.* **(6)** *Sabre briquet in scabbard.* **(7)** *Early pattern sabre briquet & scabbard.* **(8)** *Bayonet Artillerie à Pied.* **(9)** *Officers pistol.*

Straight bladed swords were usually carried on black waist belts but early on around 1804-1806 a wide white waist belt with a gilt plate embossed with a grenade surmounting crossed cannon was worn. Sword knot was gold in all cases. The officers' bicorne had a gold cockade strap and gold stiffeners and tassels. Full dress plume was scarlet and on service a scarlet pom-pon was worn, although the colonel had a white plume in a gilt holder. Cords were usually not carried in service dress. Footwear consisted of plain black hussar boots or with mounted officers heavy cavalry riding boots. Grey trousers would be worn in many instances on campaign. A gilt gorget was normally worn around the neck of officers with a silver device of crossed cannon and grenade, sometimes with a laurel leaf motive and the regimental number embossed on the centre.

In *tenue de ville* the bicorne was worn with the usual coat and white waistcoat, breeches and stockings. Black buckled shoes were worn. Horse furniture for mounted officers consisted of a blue saddle cloth, white leather saddle and blue pistol holster hoods. Horse strappings and reins were of black leather.

Artillery Train of the guard (Train d'Artillerie de la Garde)

The uniform worn in the early part of the period by this corps was a *habit coat* with short tails. The material was steel grey, that is the cloth was woven from blue and white thread. Pointed lapels were dark blue and piped in scarlet, as were the collars, pointed cuffs and turnbacks. No decoration appeared on the turnbacks. White metal buttons were used throughout. Pockets were piped scarlet and were three-pointed and vertical. Waistcoat was white and a whitened leather waist belt supported a sabre briquet. Buff skin breeches with heavy riding boots were worn. Scarlet trefoil shoulder straps were carried on the shoulders. A black bicorne with white metal stiffeners, white cockade strap, and scarlet plume was worn.

In 1806 the artillery train adopted the shako. This was black with the top band scarlet and with scarlet cords and flounders on the right side. Brass shako plates consisting of crowned eagles over crossed cannons, usually with an oblong plate beneath were worn beneath the cockade. Also in 1806 scarlet grenades appeared on the turnbacks of the coat and blue shoulder straps, piped scarlet were worn on the march. In 1807 the vertical pockets had soubise piping added (see Plate P5).

Before 1808 no pouch was worn, but that year a black leather pouch supported on a white stitched shoulder belt was introduced. The flap was embossed with a brass eagle over crossed cannon (see Plate P).

In 1809 the uniform underwent a major change when steel grey waistcoats, braided in scarlet and with three rows of white metal buttons were introduced (plate P5). At the same time steel grey hussar breeches were introduced with scarlet Hungarian knots and stripes, and hussar pattern boots trimmed and tasseled scarlet. On the march or on campaign, skin breeches or steel grey *pantalons à cheval*, with black leather inserts and 18 metal buttons (no stripe) down each leg would be worn. The shako would be covered by a black oilskin and a scarlet pom-pon replaced the plume. In 1811 the scarlet trefoils began to be progressively replaced by scarlet epaulettes.

In 1812 *habit vestes* were introduced, shown in Plate P5. The full dress wear had dark blue lapels and collars, and square cuffs piped scarlet. Cuff slashes were steel grey piped scarlet. The false turnbacks were also dark blue piped scarlet with scarlet grenades.

Around 1813 the Hungarian breeches and boots previously worn gave way to the skin breeches and high boots. For service wear a single breasted coatee similar to the Chasseurs' *Habit Kinski* was worn. This had nine white metal buttons and was piped scarlet down the front and along the straight bottom. The cuffs were pointed, dark blue, and piped in scarlet. Other details were as for the *habit veste*. In 1813 the full dress shako was covered with steel grey cloth and the *rosaces* (attachments for the chin scales) were shaped as crowns (Plate P5).

On the march or on campaign steel grey breeches were worn with the high boots. A single breasted steel grey blouse was worn on the march around 1812 with no decoration except for shoulder straps and these were plain steel grey. The blouse fastened with nine white metal buttons and the round cuffs with one white metal button. Either steel grey breeches or *pantalons à cheval* were worn with the blouse. Stable wear consisted of a long sleeved vest with dark blue collar and round cuffs. The forage cap was steel grey, piped and laced scarlet with a scarlet grenade (Plate P5). The stable dress was completed by long steel grey trousers.

The detail differences in the full dress *habit veste* of the 2nd regt, formed in 1813. Shako was plain black without peak binding and with a steel grey *lentile* disc pom-pon.

By 1810 the sabre was carried on a shoulder strap developed from the waist belt and called *ceinturon baudrier*. Saddles were of chestnut leather without a saddle cloth but with a squared

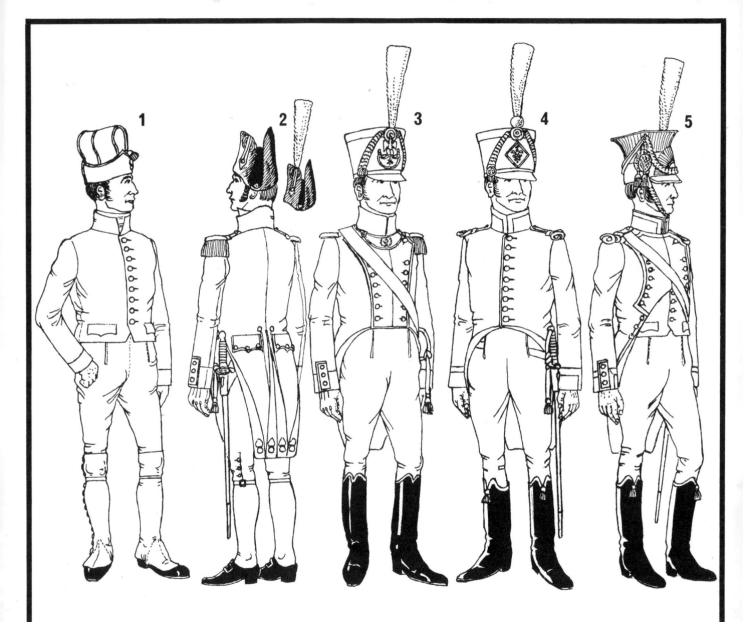

ARTILLERIE À PIED DE LIGNE: *(1) Cannonier, Tenue d'Exercice. (2) Officer, Tenue de Ville. (3) Officer, Tenue de Service. (4) Musician, 1810-12. (5) Musician, 9th Regt, 1811-12.*

portmanteau of steel grey laced scarlet (Plate P6). The steel grey double breasted greatcoat with cape was carried on top. A short barrelled musket was carried muzzle down in a bucket on the right hand side of the saddle, with a retaining strap around the small of the butt and attaching to the saddle. The butt rested on the rider's right leg. Drivers and trumpeters did not, however, carry this.

Trumpeters

The uniform worn by the trumpeters was, until 1808 identical to that worn by the trumpeters of the Guard Horse Artillery and the reader is referred to that section for information.

Full dress wear for the period 1809-1811 was as follows. A shako covered with crimson cloth was worn with the top band edged with silver lace. It had mixed silver and crimson cords and flounders. The shako plate was silver and the plume white. A *habit coat* was worn made of sky blue cloth. The collar and pointed lapels were dark blue piped crimson. Inside the crimson piping was silver lace. A silver trefoil shoulder strap was worn on the right shoulder and was lined with crimson. The turnbacks and soudisse pockets were piped crimson and silver grenades appeared on the turnbacks. On the left shoulder a mixed silver and crimson aiguillette was worn. A sky blue waistcoat with mixed silver and crimson braid and lace was worn, and sky blue Hungarian style breeches with side lacing and Hungarian knots of mixed silver and crimson. Silver and crimson piping decorated the tops of the hussar style boots. The trumpet cords were mixed silver and sky blue.

From 1812-1814 the same style uniform as that of the Horse Artillery trumpeters was again worn for full dress.

For service dress a coat similar to that described for the 1809-1811 period was worn but in place of all reference to silver read gold. In place of a shako, a black fur colpack was worn without a flap or a plume. Instead of Hungarian breeches, *pantalons à cheval* were worn. These were made of sky blue cloth and re-inforced with black leather. The outer seams were covered by a dark blue stripe upon which were 18 brass buttons.

For use with all the previously described uniforms, the shabraque was sky blue edged with scarlet lace and piped with sky blue. The valisse was also sky blue with scarlet lacing on the ends (see Plate P6).

Officers' uniform

Officers wore the same uniform as the men but in some cases (at least early on) long tailed coats were worn. Epaulettes and contra epaulettes were silver as was the shako top band and cords. The turnback grenades were also silver.

The Hungarian boots were trimmed and tasselled in silver. The pouch belt was red edged with silver and the pouch was black with silver edging and silver embossed eagle and cannon. Officers' shabraques were steel grey with a silver stripe and grenade. No valise was carried.

Line Artillery Train
(Train d'Artillerie de Ligne)

There are many conflicting contemporary descriptions of the Train uniforms but we have tried to present the widely accepted examples.

The uniform of the Line Artillery Train personnel was basically the same steel grey colour of the Guard Train. The *habit coat* with short tail was steel grey, with blue or steel grey piping and facing as shown. All breeches were of an off-white, creamy coloured skin, and heavy cavalry boots were worn. From 1804 to 1806 a bicorne was worn with a white cockade strap and a short plume of a carrot shaped pom-pom with the top half scarlet and the lower half steel grey.

A black leather pouch was carried on a whitened leather shoulder belt worn over the left shoulder, probably with crossed brass cannon on the flap. A whitened leather waist belt supported the short sabre and was fastened by a large brass buckle.

From 1808 to 1810 and also from 1812 to 1813 the *habit coat* had pointed lapels and additional soubisse piping behind the three-pointed pockets (plate P5). Other details of the dress remained the same except that the short sabre was now usually carried on the waist belt worn over the right shoulder (*ceinturon baudrier*). The brass plate on this appeared just below the heart. Elite companies appear to have worn a white grenade on the turnbacks and red pom-pons, some with a tuft.

The shako introduced in 1807 had black leather chevrons on the sides. For full dress wear, steel grey plaited cords and flounders were worn, with a steel grey plume rising from a pom-pon. Alternatively, the plume could have a blue lower half and

TRAIN D'ARTILLERIE DE LA GARDE: *(1) Driver, 1808-9. Note the long service stripe on left arm. (2) Soldat, 1810.*

pom-pon, with a scarlet top half. White cords are also indicated by some sources. The shako plate, of white metal, usually consisted of a crowned eagle over a rectangular plate bearing the battalion number as shown in the drawing. In service dress no cords were worn on the shako and a flat *lentile* disc of steel grey with the battalion number in black in the centre or a steel grey pom-pon was worn. Chin scales were of white metal.

Also in service dress, grey breeches would be worn over the skin breeches, fastening at the sides with cloth covered buttons. The greatcoat was steel grey with a short cape over the shoulder.

In 1810 the steel grey uniform was replaced by a sky blue uniform in two forms. One was the *habit coat* with blue collar, lapels and straps were sky blue piped white and the soubisse piping, three pointed pockets, and turnback grenades were also white. Waistcoat was also white and the breeches were of skin. The other coat was a chasseur pattern (*Habit Kinski*), single breasted with nine buttons down the front, shown in Plate P5.

Also from 1810, white plaited cords were worn on the shako which now in some cases had a white metal lozenge plate. A steel grey *houpette* with a white centre bearing a black battalion number was worn. On service or campaign, the shako was covered by a black oilskin and grey over trousers with black leather inserts on the inside legs worn. At the sides white metal buttons rode on a scarlet stripe.

In 1812 the *habit veste* was issued to the Train d'Artillerie in steel grey, the steel grey *habit coat* returning in 1812 also. The new coat had dark blue collar, lapels, cuffs and turnbacks, all piped steel grey and steel grey pointed shoulder straps piped blue buttoning at the shoulder instead of at the neck.

For service dress any of the following types of overall could be worn: grey with a blue stripe on the outside seams and grey cloth buttons, fawny grey without a stripe, or mid brown with cloth buttons. The field service cap was either steel grey piped blue or sky blue piped white depending on the period.

Tenue d'Ecurie (stable dress) consisted of the service cap with a long sleeved waistcoat, either steel grey with blue collar and cuffs and double breasted with two rows of 10 buttons, or in 1810 sky blue with collar and cuffs the same. In 1812 it reverted to steel grey but single breasted and with steel grey collar and cuffs. Trousers were of a coarse material, off white in colour.

Brigadiers (corporals) wore the same uniform as the men with two white stripes above each cuff. Sergeants and sergeant majors wore one or two silver stripes and it is possible that until 1812 a long tailed *habit coat* may have been worn. Corporals and sergeants certainly in many instances carried a light cavalry sabre suspended from a white waist belt in a steel scabbard.

Trumpeters wore the same uniform as the men but with the colours reversed. That is to say, where the colour was steel grey for the men, it was dark blue for the trumpeters. Additionally the collar, lapels and cuffs were laced silver. Trumpet cord was mixed white and steel grey, or plain white.

All the men, except for drivers and trumpeters, carried a cavalry musket slung butt down on the left hand side of the saddle. Horse furniture consisted of a white half sheepskin over a chestnut French saddle with a small horse cloth at the rear. A square portmanteau was carried with the greatcoat folded on top.

Officers wore the same dress as the men but usually with long tails. Rank epaulettes were silver as were the grenades on the turnbacks and it is probable that the waistcoat was white. The shako had silver cords and flounders and a steel grey plume tipped scarlet rose from a silver holder. The pouch belt was of red leather, edged with silver and the pouch was of black leather edged with silver. A light cavalry sabre was carried on a white waist belt with a brass plate. The scabbard was steel and the sword knot and hilt silver.

Officers had a square saddle cloth of steel grey with a white French saddle. The pistol hoods were also steel grey. Both the saddle cloth and hoods were laced silver.

Equipment Train (Train des Equipages)

The Equipment Train was perhaps one of the most complex of organisations with men detached to various corps all over Europe. Some mounted, some on foot, some purely workmen of various trades. The descriptions which follow give a good guide to the uniforms but there is little surviving information on the officers or trumpeters. With the officers one can assume that the same dress as the men was worn with silver rank marking, long tailed coats, etc, and for the trumpeters perhaps reversed colours.

Between 1804 and 1806 the uniform was chocolate brown with grey pointed lapels, pointed cuffs and collar. Buttons were white metal and the turnbacks steel grey without decoration.

The waistcoat was steel grey and the breeches chocolate brown. Heavy cavalry boots were worn. The black bicorne had white stiffeners and a white cockade strap. A short scarlet plume rose from the cockade. A short sabre was carried on a white waist belt with a plain rectangular brass plate.

TRAIN D'ARTILLERIE DE LA GARDE: *(1) Soldat in Tenue de Route, 1812. Note covered shako and pantalons à cheval. (2) Soldat, 1st Regt, Tenue d'Ecurie, 1813-14.*

From 1807 the shako was worn, plain black without cords but with white metal chin scales and a white metal eagle plate, with a rectangular bottom. The plume appear to have been chocolate brown with a pom-pon and the top half of the plume scarlet. Steel grey pom-pons were worn on service or later chocolate brown.

At this time the short tailed coat was also introduced (Plate P5). A white waistcoat was worn and light buff, creamy skin breeches with heavy cavalry boots. A pouch of black leather was now carried on the waistbelt which was worn over the right shoulder. In some cases a carbine belt was worn so one must assume that the light carbine was issued though the dragoon musket was more usual.

In 1812 when the *habit veste* was issued (Plate P5), the colours stayed the same but the cuffs were now square cut. The brass plate on the *ceinturon baudrier* was either plain or carried a crowned 'N'. After 1812 in fact some uniforms carried a crowned 'N' in steel grey on the turnbacks. In *tenue de route* or *service*, either brown breeches with cloth covered buttons and high boots were worn or else long overalls with black leather inserts of steel grey with a brown stripe and 16 white metal buttons riding on it (Plate P5). Additionally overalls with only brown piping down the edge and white metal buttons forward of the piping could be seen. In this case the black leather extended around the bottom six inches of the leg completely.

A *surtout*, with nine white metal buttons, brown collar, turnbacks, pointed cuffs, and pocket piping was also worn, perhaps more usually by NCOs. Stable dress consisted of the service cap, either the pointed Dragoon type or the circular 'Pokalem' (after 1812) in steel grey, piped brown, a long-sleeved waistcoat of steel grey and trousers in an off-white material. The waistcoat probably had the collar and cuffs of brown but may have been entirely steel grey. The greatcoat, three-quarter length with a cape, was steel grey and in *tenue de marche* the shako had a black oilskin cover.

Ouvriers of the train, formed in 1809, wore a single breasted coatee of steel grey or sky blue with nine or ten buttons of white metal, with the collar and pointed cuffs of dark blue, three-pointed pockets and turnbacks with white stars. Their shakos had white metal lozenge plates and red pom-pons. Service cap was steel grey or sky blue piped brown. Short black gaiters were worn. The élite company was distinguished by sky blue full epaulettes and white grenades on the turnbacks. Infantry pouches, sabre briquet and bayonet and infantry muskets were carried.

TRAIN D'ARTILLERIE DE LIGNE: *(1) Driver in cloak; breeches had red stripe with metal buttons stitched down seam. (2) Driver, 1810-11 in Habit Kinski. The coat was sky blue.*

Around 1813 a *habit veste* of steel grey with brown collar, lapels, turnbacks and shoulder strap piping was introduced together with long trousers of steel grey. Equipment was unaltered.

Brigadiers and sergeants were distinguished by two white stripes, edged brown for the brigadier, and one or two stripes in silver, edged brown for the sergeants and sergeant majors. These ranks carried a light cavalry sabre.

Horse furniture on work horses consisted of a plain French saddle in chestnut leather without any form of saddle cloth but with a square portmanteau of steel grey laced at the ends with white and with the greatcoat folded on top.

On horses used by corporals and sergeants a half sheepskin, vandyked steel grey or brown, and a saddle cloth laced white, were worn with the square portmanteau.

Medical service (Service de Santé)

The *Service de Santé* was made up of medical officers and attendants, who manned the ambulances.

Doctors appear to have worn a blue *surtout* with strips of gold lace across the chest level with the nine buttons. The blue collar

APPENDIX 1: IMPERIAL LIVERY

In 1812 Napoleon decreed that all drummers and trumpeters would wear his Imperial lace, thus tending to standardise the former gaudy uniforms used. The lace was worn on a dark Imperial green coat with facing variations to suit individual regiments (see specific regiments for details). The lace was of two types, one for use vertically and one for use horizontally. This was yellow, edged scarlet with black dividers separating alternate eagles and 'N's in green. The eagles and 'N's were always upright, this being the main difference between the horizontal and vertical versions. A form of lace rarely seen had green eagles on a yellow background and yellow 'N's on a green background; otherwise it was almost identical to the lace previously described. Where two rows of lace appeared together (eg, across the chest), they were separated by a white cord with the end fringed.

had two strips of gold lace at each side of the front running horizontally. Cuffs appear to have been round with three lace strips on which brass buttons appeared. A sword with a brass hilt was worn in a steel scabbard. Breeches would be blue with turned down boots or grey *pantalons à cheval* with brass buttons down the sides. A bicorne was worn with gold cockade straps. Horse furniture consisted of a square saddle cloth of blue, laced gold with a fawn French saddle. Double holster hoods were also blue, laced gold and the horse strappings were black.

Infirmiers (medical attendants) wore a short tailed *habit coat* of brown with the collar, pointed lapels, pointed cuffs and turnbacks scarlet piped white. Shakos were black with lozenge plates of white metal as were the chin straps. A red pom-pon was worn over the cockade. Full equipment consisted of a sabre briquet, infantry style pouch, fawny red haversack and a steel grey greatcoat rolled on top. The infantry musket was also carried. Breeches were white and short black gaiters were worn. In many cases a canvas belt was worn around the waist, under the coat with buttons along the top edge forming a waist pouch. Medical aids were carried in this waist pouch.

In 1812 the *habit coat* was adopted but the colours remained the same.

APPENDIX 2: TABLE OF EQUIVALENT RANKS

French		British
Colonel	} Senior Officers {	Colonel
Major		Lieutenant Colonel
Chef d'Escadron		Major
Capitaine		Captain
Lieutenant		Lieutenant
Adjutant		Warrant Officer
Marechal des Logis Chef	Sous }	Sergeant Major
Marechal des Logis	Officiers }	Sergeant
Brigadier/Corporal		Corporal
Cannonier 1me Classe }		Bombardier/Lance Corporal
Ouvrier 1me Classe }		
Tambour Major		Drum Major
Trompette Major		Trumpet Major
Brigadier Trompette		Corporal Trumpeter
Trompette		Trumpeter
Tambour		Drummer
Soldat		Soldier (ie, Private

APPENDIX 3: ARTILLERY STANDARDS

Standards were only carried by the Artillery regiments, not by the Train. The flags of the Horse Artillery, both Guard and Line were in the shape of guidons with rounded shallow tails until 1812 (fig 1). The guidon carried a white lozenge with the corners running from the top, next to the staff, blue, then scarlet (outer top), blue (lower outer) and scarlet (lower next to staff).

Each of these corners carried a circlet of laurel leaves with ribbons in the centre of which appeared a hunting horn for the Guard and the regimental number in the case of the Line.

The white lozenge was edged with a leaf design and the following gold lettering was carried on the white. In the case of the Guard:

L'EMPEREUR
DES FRANCAIS
AU REGT D'ARTILLERIE
A CHEVAL
DE LA GARDE
IMPERIAL

on the reverse appeared a crowned eagle flanked by the gold lettering **VALEUR ET DISCIPLINE** and below the emblem 2me ESCADRON or as appropriate to the individual unit.

The line regiments were lettered as follows:

L'EMPEREUR
DES FRANCAIS
AU 1re REGIMENT
D'ARTILLERIE
A CHEVAL

The reverse was the same as the Guard but without the eagle and laid out as follows:

VALEUR
ET DISCIPLINE
2me ESCADRON

The Regiments à Pied (Foot), both Guard and Line followed the same layout but with square flags instead of guidons.

In 1813 most flags were changed to a tricolour (fig 2) with the regimental title as before on the face and the battle honours on the reverse. The flagstaffs were blue and were surmounted by the Imperial bronze eagle.

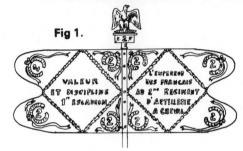

Fig 1.

Typical Horse or Guard Artillery guidon prior to 1812.

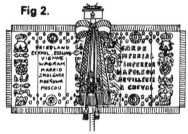

Fig 2.

Typical Horse or Guard Artillery guidon from 1813, based on the national tricolour.

Rank Distinctions: Officers

RANK	HORSE ARTILLERY —GUARD (1) (2)	FOOT ARTILLERY —GUARD	HORSE ARTILLERY —LINE (1) (2)	FOOT ARTILLERY —LINE	TRAIN d'ARTILLERIE —GUARD	TRAIN d'ARTILLERIE —LINE	TRAIN d'EQUIPAGE
Colonel	Five stripes on sleeves and breeches 3 of 14mm and 2 of 23mm gold lace	2 full epaulettes of heavy gold bullion	As Guard	As Guard Foot	——	——	——
Adjutant	——	——	——	As Colonel Guard Foot but with shoulder strap of silver	——	——	——
Major	As Colonel but centre stripe of silver lace	As Adjutant of Line regts	As Guard	Full epaulette on left. Contra epaulette on right. Heavy gold bullion	——	——	——
Chef d' Escadron (Chef d' Battalion for Foot)	Four gold stripes alternate 14 and 23mm Starting with 14mm on the cuff	As Major of Line regts	As Guard	——	——	——	——

Rank Distinctions: Officers

RANK	HORSE ARTILLERY —GUARD (1) (2)	FOOT ARTILLERY —GUARD	HORSE ARTILLERY —LINE (1) (2)	FOOT ARTILLERY —LINE	TRAIN d'ARTILLERIE —GUARD	TRAIN d'ARTILLERIE —LINE	TRAIN d'EQUIPAGE
Capitaine	2 of 14mm wide with 1 of 23mm between	As Major Line Regt but with fine bullion	As Guard	As Guard Foot	As Guard Foot but silver in place of gold		
Lieutenant	2 of 14mm	As Capitaine but with a thin red stripe along shoulder strap	As Guard	As Guard Foot	As Guard Foot but silver in place of gold		
Sous-Lieutenant	1 of 14mm	As Capitaine but with a red lozenge on straps	As Guard	As Guard Foot	As Guard Foot but silver in place of gold		

NOTES:
(1) See Illustration.
(2) On the sleeves, the first 14mm lace appeared on the cuff itself. All braid and lacing was gold. Pelisse had white or grey fur.

Rank Distinctions: NCOs and other ranks

RANK	HORSE ARTILLERY —GUARD	FOOT ARTILLERY —GUARD	HORSE ARTILLERY —LINE	FOOT ARTILLERY —LINE	TRAIN d'ARTILLERIE —GUARD	TRAIN d'ARTILLERIE —LINE	TRAIN d'EQUIPAGES
Sergeant-Major (Marechal des Logis Chefs)	Two inverted gold lace chevrons above each cuff 1	Two gold lace stripes at an angle above each cuff. Piped scarlet 4	As Guard Horse 1 7	As Guard Foot 8	As Guard Horse but silver lace piped scarlet	As Guard Foot but silver lace 9	As Guard Train but piped chocolate brown
Sergeant (Marechal des Logis)	As Sergeant-Major but only one chevron 1	As Sergeant-Major but only one stripe 4	As Guard Horse 1 7	As Guard Foot 8	As Guard Horse but silver lace piped scarlet	As Guard Foot but silver lace 9	As Guard Train but piped chocolate brown
Brigadier (Corporal)	Two inverted chevrons above each cuff of aurore wool 2	Two stripes of aurore wool over each cuff 5	As Guard Horse but yellow wool	As Guard Foot	As Guard Horse but scarlet	As Guard Foot but white	As Guard Train but white piped chocolate brown
Gunners 1st Class	As for Corporal but worn on left cuff only	As for Corporals but worn on left cuff only 6	As Guard Horse but yellow wool	As Guard Foot	—	—	—
Long Service Stripes (Worn on left upper sleeve)	Gold for NCOs Aurore for Corporal and Men 3	Gold for NCOs Aurore for Corporals and Men 3	Gold for NCOs Scarlet for Corporals and Men 3	Gold for NCOs Scarlet for Corporals and Men 3	—	—	—

NOTES:
1 All lace on dolman, pelisse and breeches was of mixed scarlet and gold in ratio 2 scarlet to 1 gold. Fur on pelisse (where applicable) was fawn. When coat was worn the aiguillette was mixed scarlet and gold, and the trefoil shoulder strap was gold on a scarlet patch. Turnback grenades were gold.
2 Aurore was an orangey-salmon colour.
3 One for ten years, two for 15 years, and three for 20-25 years.
4 Bearskin grenade was gold as were the turnback grenades. Cords on shako or bearskin mixed scarlet and gold. Shako had top band of gold lace. Epaulettes had scarlet straps, edged gold with gold crescents and mixed scarlet and gold fringes.
5 Also Maitre Ouvriers of the work battalion.
6 Also Ouvriers 1st Classe.
7 Top band of shako of gold lace. Epaulettes had scarlet straps edged gold, gold crescents and mixed scarlet and gold fringes.
8 Sometimes piped scarlet. Where epaulettes were worn details as Guard.
9 Often wore long tailed coats.

APPENDIX 4: ALPHABETICAL GLOSSARY OF TERMS AND ORDERS OF DRESS

Aiguillettes A cord shoulder strap with an ornamental knot from which loops of plain and plaited cords hung, fastening to a lapel buttonhole or to the chest.

Barrel Sash A waist sash worn with Hussar style uniforms passing through 'barrels' of a contrasting colour. It secured at the back by a wooden toggle and loop. Two cords went to the front fastening and ended in tassels.

Bicorne A broad brimmed hat with the edges turned up on two opposite sides.

Bonnet de Police A cloth service cap or fatigue cap usually with a pointed top flap which was usually tucked into the side. See Pokalem.

Brass Napoleonic period brass normally had a high content of copper and therefore had a distinctly reddish appearance. Yellow brass was also used however.

Brandenburgs Lace edging to buttonholes, usually with a fringe.

Breeches Tight fitting trousers.

Carbine A short barreled musket carried by most mounted troops.

Carbine belt A leather shoulder belt with a swivel hook that attached to a ring which was carried in a slide on the carbine.

Chevrons 'V' shaped laces indicative of rank or service.

Cockade A rosette which varied in colouring and layers or rings and which denoted nationality. The French cockade was blue centre, red, then white outer.

Colpack A round fur busby usually with a 'bag' or flap on the top.

Contra epaulette An epaulette without fringes.

Cuff slash Oblong patch on round cuffs which closed the cuff fastening with three buttons. They could be plain or have one side with three points.

Czapska Lancer cap of Polish origin with a square flap top.

Dolman A tight fitting jacket of Hussar pattern with braiding across the chest.

Epaulette A shoulder strap with fringed ends.

Flounders (Raquettes, Fr.) Flat woven oval shaped decorations with tassels that were suspended by cords usually from headgear.

Gaiters Cloth leg coverings. Fastened with buttons on the outer side and with a strap and buckle above the knee.

Girth Wide band which held the saddle in place.

Grand tenue Full dress.

Habit coat Long or short tailed coat with a cutaway front.

Habit Kinski This was a garment introduced in the 1810-12 period. It was a single breasted coatee fastened by nine buttons. It had piping in the appropriate colour down the front and along the bottom edge.

Habit veste Short tailed coat with a straight cut waist at the front.

Howitzer A high trajectory weapon.

Hungarian knots Elaborate braiding of interwoven circles on the front of Hussar style breeches.

Hussar boots Soft leather boots curving up at the front and rear with a 'V' notch cut out at the front and a tassel sometimes hanging from the front.

Lentile A flattened disc of wool worn in place of a plume.

Musket A smooth bore flint lock firearm usually with a bayonet attachment.

Pantalons à cheval Trousers usually worn over the breeches to protect them. These were of various patterns, usually with coloured (or sometimes gold) lace and buttons down the outer seams depending on the arm or unit.

Pelisse A fur trimmed jacket usually carried over the shoulders but worn in place of the dolman in inclement weather.

Piping A raised tubular length of material decorating the edges of pockets, cuffs, etc.

Pistol hoods Carriers on the front of the saddle. Usually of two or three layers and decorated in the same fashion as the saddle cloth.

Pockets There are various styles of pockets the main types being three pointed either vertical or horizontal.

Pointed lapels Lapels which at the bottom followed the cutaway of the coat merging at the edge.

Pointed cuffs Cuffs which rose to point and buttoned at the rear usually with one button on the cuff and the other above.

Pokalem cap High, round cap with flap which could be let down and buttoned under chin.

Pom-pon A spherical ball of wool worn in place of a plume.

Saddlecloth Usually a square cut cloth worn under the saddle sometimes with pointed rear ends hanging down.

Sabretache A leather case usually with a coloured cloth face, suspended on three straps from the sword belt.

Sapeur Equivalent of the British 'pioneer'. Carried an axe and wore a leather apron.

Shabraque A horse cloth which covered the saddle and usually had pointed rear ends.

Shako Headgear with peak made of leather and felt.

Sous officier Senior NCO.

Square cuffs Cuffs which turned back equally all round the sleeve. Usually with a cuff slash.

Square lapels Lapels on a cutaway coat that ended at the bottom at 90° to the cutaway.

Surtout Single breasted garment without lapels, buttoning at the front usually with nine buttons.

Sword knot Strap on the hilt of a sword which passed around the wrist in action to prevent loss.

Tenue de campaign Dress worn on active service.

Tenue d'ecurie Stable dress.

Tenue de marche Dress worn on the march.

Tenue de ville Walking out or town dress.

Vandyking Triangular cut edging usually to a sheepskin saddle cloth.

Velites Recruits or trainees.